Pressure groups and government in Great Britain

CONTENTS

PREFACE

This book had its immediate origins in a leisurely conversation between myself and Professor Bernard Crick which took place at Birkbeck College, London, in August 1981. The conversation, as I recall, ranged over a great many topics which interested the two of us concerning developments in modern British public administration. To my surprise Professor Crick asked me to draft a synopsis for a monograph on pressure groups and the governing process in Britain. Within a matter of weeks Longman had agreed to publish the work.

All my writings on modern British politics have been coloured by a personal approach which aims to preserve objectivity without sacrificing conviction. This is especially true of the book I now present to my readers. It is neither a textbook nor a guidebook, but rather a 'view' of the role of pressure groups in the British system of government. Its starting point is the belief that, while aspects of this role certainly give cause for concern, pressure groups are neither sinister nor subversive; they are facts of political life as necessary to the good ordering of society as the Cabinet or the Houses of Parliament.

The August 1981 meeting between Professor Crick and myself was originally intended to explore a quite different literary matter, in which Professor Crick's interest and concern were a great source of encouragement and comfort. The thanks I now offer him therefore extend beyond those due in respect of the present work.

Dr Geoffrey Alderman
Royal Holloway College
University of London

ACKNOWLEDGEMENTS

I wish to place on record my appreciation of the help given by the following individuals and organizations during the research for this book:
Action on Smoking and Health; The Association of British Chambers of Commerce; The Automobile Association; Dr Rodney Barker; The British Boxing Board of Control (1929); The Building Societies Association; The Cabinet Office; The Civil Service Department; The Confederation of British Industry; John Gorst, MP; The Home Office; The Institute of Directors; Eric Moonman; The National Chamber of Trade; The National Farmers Union; The National Union of Teachers; The Parliamentary and Scientific Committee; Paul Winner Marketing Communications Limited (Paul Winner); Political Research and Communication International Limited (Douglas Smith); The Public Relations Consultants Association (Marie Jennings); The Royal Automobile Club; The Royal Society for the Prevention of Cruelty to Animals.

A number of civil servants were kind enough to give me interviews and information on a non-attributable basis.

To A. F. Thompson

Chapter one
HISTORY

This book is about pressure groups in Great Britain. The territorial limitation is deliberate. I have not engaged in an exercise in comparative government. And, mainly from a deep sense of academic inadequacy, I have deliberately avoided dealing with Northern Ireland. Whatever view one takes of public affairs in that unhappy province, there can be no doubt that in Northern Ireland consensus on the most basic issues of government has broken down, if indeed it ever existed: that is, there is no general unanimity of view on what form the institutions of government in Northern Ireland should take. My concern is with Great Britain – England, Scotland and Wales – where there is general agreement on the shape of the basic components of the machinery of government and where, therefore, pressure groups operate in a consensual framework even though, as we shall see, there is much disagreement about the precise place of pressure groups within that framework.

But 'pressure groups'. What are they? The very term has a sinister ring about it. The American word 'lobby' is no more endearing. In nineteenth-century America 'lobbies' were widespread, while in England 'interests' grew apace. Learned tomes have been written concerning the distinction between interests, lobbies and pressure groups, and political theorists have delighted in feats of verbal dexterity aimed at arriving at precise definitions of, and pointing to precise differences between, each of them (Wootton 1970:1–44). Indeed, if we wish to travel down this road we might note that the editors of a collection of essays on British pressure groups list no less than twenty-one terms they have found in 'group' literature (Kimber and Richardson 1974a:1).

As if this were not enough, a completely new science of pressure-group theory has been invented in the United States of America and exported to this country. When in 1969 I submitted for examination at Oxford a doctoral thesis on the railway interest in the United Kingdom in the late nineteenth and early twentieth centuries, one of my examiners (the late Kenneth Tite, of Magdalen College) gently berated me for having omitted to mention the American journalist Arthur F. Bentley. The thesis was accepted, the omission notwithstanding. The criticism was both just and irrelevant. Bentley, a Chicago newspaperman, published in 1908 a book entitled *The Process of Government.* He believed, correctly, that books then existing which endeavoured to explain the working of American government concentrated narrowly upon institutions, such as the Congress and the Presidency. He was far more interested in the dynamics of government, in politics 'in the raw'. And from his observation of American government Bentley concluded that the entire governmental process revolved around groups. This led Bentley (1967:269) to formulate a dictum that has since become famous:

> All phenomena of government are phenomena of groups pressing one another, forming one another and pushing out new groups and group representatives (the organs or agencies of government) to mediate the adjustments.

Government itself, Bentley claimed, was the creation of interest groups and, having been created, became a group participating in inter-group activity, now working on behalf of one set of interests, now working on behalf of another. Nor was the party political process exempt from this dynamic. Bentley (1967:401) wrote:

> Parties may be found which are best to be described as the special organization for political activity of interest groups, especially of classes, direct. Others are the organization in a representative degree of a set of such interest groups.

It is really no exaggeration to say that Bentley believed that the process of government *was* the process of group interaction. 'When the groups are adequately stated, everything is stated. When I say everything I mean everything.' (Bentley 1967:208–9)

Bentley's work certainly was an antidote to stodgy institutional and narrowly constitutional studies of government, in America and elsewhere. But in his analysis of the workings of government he was saying nothing new. Man eschews loneliness. The ancient Israelites roamed the desert in groups (tribes). Jesus of Nazareth had his apostles. The feudal system which flourished in England between the eleventh and the fourteenth centuries was, among other things, a system of government in which the relationship between each group in society, and the rights and obligations of each towards the other, was strictly ordered, and generally based upon land tenure. The English Civil War was an armed struggle between groups rather than individuals. Bentley's view of parties (quoted above) shows that he regarded the class component of political activity as especially important. But in so doing he was merely following Karl Marx. For the entire Marxist analysis of industrial society is based on the assumption that society is composed of groups and that it is the behaviour of groups, not of individuals, that determines the force and direction of the dialectic. Moreover, whereas American group theorists believe in and allow for people being 'cross-pressured' (that is, being a member of more than one group at once, and being able to move from one group to another), Marxist theory holds that whether we are conscious of it or not, and whether we believe we are acting freely or not, our behaviour is in fact determined overwhelmingly by our class (that is, group) situation.

Socialist critiques of British society as it developed in the nineteenth century were bound, therefore, to be much concerned with group behaviour. It is no coincidence that one of the earliest surveys of pressure groups in Britain was produced by the Fabian Research Department and written by Sidney and Beatrice Webb (Webb 1917). Their examination of professional associations, published during the First World War, marks a watershed in the study of pressure groups in British government. But it was not the first such study. Bentley had clearly hoped that his essentially philosophical and methodological approach to groups would be followed by empirical studies. Seven years after the publication of *The Process of Government*, a 'special agent' of the Bureau of Foreign and Domestic Commerce in Washington produced a (somewhat inaccurate) account of British manufacturers' and employers' organizations (Wolfe 1915). This was indeed putting 'Bentleyism' into practice.

Academic observers of British government were slow to build upon these foundations. In the United States, by contrast, group theory flourished, and the systematic study of pressure groups began in earnest. It is easy to see why. Because the executive and legislative branches of American government are entirely separate, though interdependent, because each is elected by the voters as a whole for fixed terms of office, and also because party discipline, as we know it in Britain, is virtually non-existent, the executive in the United States cannot be controlled exclusively through Congress. A revolt of disgruntled Congressmen will not bring down the President, for a

President (unless, like Richard Nixon, he omits to destroy incriminating tape-recordings) is safe for a four-year term once elected.

So those who wish to influence presidential decisions must organize at Washington, and not simply rely on the Congress, even though they may have sympathetic representation within it. Equally, there is no sanction, such as the threat of a dissolution, which a President can deploy against a rebellious Congress in order to bring it to heel. He, too, must organize, cajole and persuade. The geographical expanse of the United States is also an incentive to form and act through groups, because personal contact with a Congressman or Senator is often difficult. And there is in the United States a much deeper tradition of popular participation in government even at the very lowest levels. Many individual states of the Union have referendums, and most Americans are able to elect a variety of public officials.

In short, those American citizens who wish to make any impact upon their state or federal governments must organize into groups. There is no other way. Professor Wootton traces the term 'lobbying' in the United States to the early nineteenth century. By the time of the American Civil War 'to lobby' had come to be defined as 'to address or solicit members of a legislative body in the lobby or elsewhere away from the House, with a view to influence [*sic*] their votes. This is practised by persons not belonging to the legislature' (quoted in Wootton 1975:4; the definition is that in the 1864 edition of Webster's dictionary). Several features of this definition are worthy of note. Firstly, the author of the definition was clear that lobbying was an activity directed against the legislature only. Secondly, lobbying need not take place *at* the legislature. Thirdly, the object of lobbying was to influence legislative *votes* and not, for example, to influence the conduct of legislators towards projects or causes that did not involve the casting of votes. We may note that by the mid-twentieth century the term, as used in America, had changed but little. The 1948 edition of Funk and Wagnall's *New Practical Standard Dictionary* defined lobbying as accosting, addressing or soliciting legislators or legislative bodies 'for the purpose of influencing or securing legislation advantageous to one's own interests'.

Inevitably the term 'lobby', with its derivatives, crossed the Atlantic and was absorbed into the vocabulary of British politics. Formally it has retained the restrictions its American begetters placed upon it. 'To lobby', says the *Concise Oxford Dictionary* (6th edn, 1976) is to 'seek to influence' members of a legislature, or to

'solicit' th
term can now mean merely to solicit the support of an 'influential person', whether a legislator or not.

Professor Samuel Finer, in his pioneering work on British pressure groups, declares that the term 'lobby' embraces all groups which 'seek to influence public policy', and that the chief characteristic of a lobby is its 'attempt to influence government' (Finer 1966:4–5). It is clear from the substance of Professor Finer's work that he regards the natural habitat of the lobby as being Westminster and Whitehall, the legislative and executive seats of British government. But there seems no good reason to the present author why one should not speak, nowadays, of lobbies working in the context of local government, nationalized industries, or even private enterprise. Town halls and county halls are continually lobbied. British Rail and the Post Office have to endure the lobbies too; and private firms are often lobbied on national and local issues. Whatever the strict historical origins of the term, a lobby today, in the British context, is any group which seeks to influence public policy directly, through any of the organs of government, or indirectly, through an agency which, though not itself an organ of government, is perceived as having influence over government. One may speak, for example, of a consumer group 'lobbying' for the support of the Trades Union Congress in order to obtain trade-union backing for legislative change.

It is clear from the tone with which the activity of lobbying was described by English writers in the nineteenth century – a tone varying from the apologetic to the downright contemptuous – that the term 'lobby' was felt to be foreign if not actually immoral. This was not because lobbying was not indulged in, but rather because the interdependence of the legislative and executive branches of government in Britain seemed to require a term which emphasized community of feeling and absence of tension. There was, as it happens, such a term: 'interest'. And it is in the development of interests in the eighteenth and nineteenth centuries that the true origins of the modern British pressure group are to be found.

The soliciting of government by commercial groups in Great Britain has a long history. It grew in importance, and developed political overtones, in the eighteenth century because the economic and constitutional climates were favourable to it. Exponents of the classic liberal tradition, such as Adam Smith, had followed Rousseau in believing that the *organized* pursuit of sectional or vested interests was, almost by definition, a public menace. Rousseau held that groups divide the true community or the general authoritative will;

Jeremy Bentham spoke of 'sinister interests', identifying group politics with residual feudal privilege which, he argued, prevented rational calculation by a democratic state of the sum total of individual interests, the greatest happiness of the greatest number (Beer 1969:40). But the industrial revolution led inevitably to a gradual extension of the activities of central government. The human and commercial problems to which industrialization gave rise undermined a set of beliefs which had seen virtue only in the pursuit of individual self interest (Colman 1975:11). The growth of towns and of factories created a society in which groups of people depended upon each other for their needs. Nonconformity helped foster a social conscience, and helped also to articulate it. A reasonably free press emerged to act as a focus for public discussion, and Parliament proved independent enough to take up public grievances.

Moreover, the soliciting of government by both commercial and civic groups was fostered by the doctrine of political representation then dominant, and championed by Edmund Burke, which stressed that it was the duty of a Member of Parliament to represent the interests of the whole community, and not just those of his own particular constituency and his own electors. Burke (1823:20) told the Bristol electors in 1774:

> Parliament is not a *congress* of ambassadors from different and hostile interests . . . but . . . a deliberative assembly of *one* nation . . . You choose a member indeed; but when you have chosen him, he is not member of Bristol, but he is a member of *parliament*.

Such a concept ruled out any idea of 'mandating' MPs. 'I pay no regard whatever to the voice of the people', the radical Charles James Fox declared; 'it is our duty to do what is proper without considering what may be agreeable' (quoted in Owen 1974:291). The independence of MPs, and their immunity from extra-parliamentary coercion (one of the issues fought out between the Roundheads and the Cavaliers) was thus complete. But this did not mean that MPs had a licence to do what they pleased. Their duty was to address themselves to the national interest and the national interests.

Now it was perfectly true that great borough-mongers, such as the Duke of Newcastle, controlled votes in the Commons. But this was because they were also great landowners; since the wealth of the country was (and remained until the second half of the nineteenth century) founded upon agriculture, their interests were synonymous with those of the nation as a whole. Legitimate 'interests' – that is, the social and economic groups which contributed to the nation's well-being – had every right to be represented in Parliament, and to make representations to it. Thus the political power exercised by such bodies as the East India Company and the Bank of England, power based partly upon the loyalty of a bloc of MPs and partly upon their own national importance, was accepted without question. However, *purely* extra-parliamentary organizations, such as the Yorkshire Association of 1779–80 (formed with the avowed aim of putting pressure upon MPs to achieve economical and parliamentary reform) were considered to have no legitimate interest in the well-being of the nation, and were consequently viewed with great suspicion (Hunt 1960; Beer 1957).

'Interests' abounded in British parliamentary politics in the eighteenth and nineteenth centuries. To the East India and West India interests in the eighteenth century may be added the Canal, Railway and Shipping Interests in the nineteenth. All these, and many more, shared certain common features. They could all count on the support of friendly MPs in Parliament; invariably these MPs were themselves members of the interests they defended. But the activities of the interests were all co-ordinated outside Parliament. And they all boasted, or came to boast, of formal extra-parliamentary organizations which undertook political and propaganda duties, acted as a forum for debate and for the resolution of differences, came (intentionally or otherwise) to impose upon their members a certain internal discipline, and came also to be regarded, by Parliament and government alike, as the authoritative bodies through which a dialogue with each particular interest might be maintained.

Some groups took to organizing themselves in order to maximize the pressure they could exert upon government, or upon other interests. Others found organization forced on them as the spectre of state control loomed ever larger. The West India Interest formed its own Society of West India Merchants to protect the interests of the colonies from the activities of the home government (Penson 1921). The establishment of the first British chambers of commerce, in New York and Jersey in 1768, was followed by the formation of others within the British Isles, at Glasgow and Belfast in 1783, at Edinburgh in 1785, and at Manchester in 1794. During the 1770s and 1780s important groups of manufacturers, like the Staffordshire potters and the Midland ironmasters, set up trade associations and undertook the organization of interest groups to serve their needs (Norris 1957–8:450; Read 1964:24). At this time, too, the expansion of canal-building gave ample opportunity to MPs and canal promoters to combine together for their mutual advancement (Beer

1957:625–7). Nor was it long before employers' organizations sprang up, as at Sheffield in 1814, to resist the demands of trade unions (Wolfe 1915:37).

Thus by the beginning of the railway age not only was the existence of interest groups taken for granted, but the activities of such groups, and pre-eminently of commercial groups, in the political arena were very well established. In general such activities remained local or regional, without national co-ordination. Samuel Garbett's General Chamber of Manufacturers, formed in 1785 to oppose Pitt's proposed commercial treaty with Ireland, fell apart the following year over a similar treaty with France. Only when an entire industry was threatened by government policy were concerted efforts made to organize counter-measures in and out of Parliament; in 1790, for instance the brewers set up a 'junta' in London to attend to parliamentary affairs (Mathias 1958).

Local chambers of commerce remained for much of the nineteenth century narrow-minded and inward-looking. Even the formation of the Association of British Chambers of Commerce, in 1860, had little immediate effect. The inability of many early farming organizations, such as the Farmers' Club of 1842, to mobilize support and produce acceptable results, led to the formation in 1879 of a far more militant body, the Farmers' Alliance. The British Iron Trade Association was not established till 1876. The Shipping Interest remained divided even after the formation of the Chamber of Shipping, in 1878; the Shipping Federation, organized primarily to fight trade unionism, dated only from 1890, whilst the Shipowners' Parliamentary Committee, whose task it was to look after shipping interests at Westminster, was not formed until 1893.

Generally speaking, most industries had to wait until well into the late nineteenth century, when falling profits and higher costs produced a greater sense of urgency, before they obtained national centrally-controlled representatives bodies, geared to defend them from political and governmental attack. This was even true of the 'peak' associations. The Trades Union Congress was not founded till 1868. A national organization of employers did not appear until the establishment, in 1898, of the Employers' Parliamentary Council.

Standing head and shoulders above all these, however, was the great Railway Interest. In the nineteenth-century Railway Interest one sees the interest group in its most advanced, sophisticated and ruthless form. Its roots reached deep into the economic and social fabric of the nation. It was exceedingly well represented in Parliament: between 1868 and 1906 the number of MPs with directorships of nationally important railways never fall below 20, and was often over 40 and occasionally over 50. Behind them stood the thousands of shareholders, who could be mobilized for support when required. Co-ordinating all these efforts was the Railway Companies' Association (founded in 1867 as the United Railway Companies' Committee), which continued in existence until the nationalization of the railways in 1948.

The Railway Interest was able to look governments squarely in the face. It was not afraid of challenging Parliament, or other interest groups, and it could claim important victories to its credit. Moreover, it had plenty of money at its disposal. It was, consequently, a power in the land. Thomas Farrer, Permanent Secretary at the Board of Trade, did not exaggerate when he warned the President of the Board, Joseph Chamberlain, in 1885, that 'I cannot think it will be well to make an enemy of the highly organized, lasting, deep-pocketed R[ail] W[ay] interest . . . The wrath of the Companies is red hot steel' (quoted in Alderman 1973:106). Yet, within thirty years, the Railway Interest – as distinct from the Railway Companies' Association – was to become a spent force. And the reasons for its decline help explain why the terms 'interest' and 'interest groups', while wholly appropriate in an eighteenth- or nineteenth-century context, are very inappropriate thereafter.

Of paramount importance was the growth in parliamentary party discipline, itself partly a result of the extensions of the franchise in the later nineteenth century. In order to cater for large middle-class and expanding working-class electorates, the Conservative and Liberal parties developed constituency-based extra-parliamentary organizations of mass membership: the Conservative National Union and the National Liberal Federation. Party labels acquired a much greater significance; the independent MP all but disappeared. Of course, MPs retained close links with business and commerce. But these links were not so important as they had once been. In 1911 Parliament agreed to the proposal that MPs be paid. By the outbreak of the First World War there were only a handful of MPs who were prepared to put the interests of their railway companies, or of any other business concerns with which they were connected, above the interests of their parties. In a prophetic memorandum written shortly before the First World War commenced, a senior railway administrator (probably A. B. Cane, Secretary to the Railway Companies' Association, quoted in Alderman 1973:220) warned:

> The future of the great Corporations will lie more and more in the Government offices and less in Parliament. It is hopeless to expect to influence Parliamentary majorities, who will act under prejudice when they do not act upon orders. But it may be possible to persuade administrators.

A factor of almost equal importance was that the minutiae of government regulation of industry were no longer discussed at Westminster. The real negotiations on these matters took place behind the closed doors of the great departments of state in and around Whitehall. Parliament was simply not equipped, nor did it wish, to deal with technical matters. It was, in any case, far more congenial, both for government and industry, to iron out differences in Whitehall and then come to Westminster as friends.

So it was that in a wide variety of matters concerning government policy towards industry, commerce, agriculture and the environment, as well as social questions, power passed from Members of Parliament to civil servants. The exigencies of the First World War accelerated the process. One particular catalyst of this change deserves special mention: delegated legislation, 'the statutory practice whereby Parliament empowers the Administration (generally a Minister or the Queen in Council) to make rules and regulations' (Griffith and Street 1967:4).

Examples of delegated legislation can be found in the nineteenth century, but it is essentially a twentieth-century device, justified by reference to the necessity for speed (particularly in emergencies), flexibility (in revising legislation to take account of changed circumstances) and complexity (because Parliament does not possess the necessary technical skills or specialist knowledge). The pros and cons of delegated legislation have been long and passionately debated. Lord Chief Justice Hewart wrote with eloquence against what he termed 'departmental legislation' (Hewart 1929: Ch. VI), and there have been several attempts to amend parliamentary procedure to allow for greater scrutiny of statutory instruments. For our purpose three points only need be noted. The first is that delegated legislation is here to stay; indeed, in a typical parliamentary session far more statutory instruments are approved than Bills enacted. The second is that parliamentary scrutiny of statutory instruments is, by common agreement, totally inadequate; as a result, there is a tendency for the Joint Select Committee of both Houses (established in 1973 to replace separate Committees in the Commons and the Lords) to trust the executive, so that if a government department certifies that a particular instrument is necessary, and has been drafted after full consultation with 'interested parties', Parliament is unlikely to raise any objection. The third is that although, originally, delegated legislation was meant to deal with relatively minor matters, since the Second World War some very important issues have been dealt with in this way: limited increases in national insurance contributions, closures of schools, immigration rules and Sunday trading, to name but a few (Alderman 1982; Beith 1981:166).

In 1978 the Joint Select Committee itself, in a special report, drew attention to and condemned the 'recurring tendency' of ministers and their departments to seek to by-pass Parliament by making statutory instruments which omitted details the public had a right to know about, or which left the way open for wide ministerial discretion (*The Times* 9 Feb. 1978:2). But there are no signs that this tendency has diminished. Delegated legislation has consequently moved the arena of discussion away from Westminster and into Whitehall, where technical know-how and negotiating skills are much more important than parliamentary expertise. The great interest groups which in many respects dominated and in a few actually controlled British political debate in the eighteenth and nineteenth centuries are no more. The term has, however, survived in a variety of curious ways, partly, no doubt, because all members of a particular group may be assumed to be 'interested' in the group's objectives, and to have a stake in the position which it seeks to defend or enhance. Professor Finer's definition of interest groups – 'economic associations which exercise political power . . . [and] . . . politically active groups which exercise economic power' (Finer 1958:2) – seems unduly narrow, and its insistence on the exercise of 'power' makes it at once suspect and exclusive. The Lord's Day Observance Society, for instance, was, a hundred years ago, a potent interest group, and in some respects is still not without influence; but it is not an economic association and does not exercise – and has never exercised – 'power' (Wigley 1980). We might also note that the members of an interest group need not themselves benefit from the objectives they seek to advance; the activities of the Anti-Slavery Society, past and present, indicate the strength of this maxim.

In these circumstances it seems safer to consign the term 'interest group' to the history books. Interest groups were the children of a particular parliamentary system, and they disappeared as that system was swept away. But side-by-side with them there developed an altogether different sort of group, which displayed some characteristics of an interest group and some of a lobby, but whose attentions were certainly not directed merely towards the legislature. It is in these groups that the direct lineal descendants of modern British pressure groups are to be found.

In size, membership and specialism these groups differed radically one from another. Some were professional associations, whose members were concerned primarily to enhance the status of their profession and to limit entry into it by prescribing the qualifications necessary for membership and by being able to exclude from it those who were adjudged to have brought it into disrepute. Thus the Incorporated Law Society, formed in 1825, was empowered by the 1888 Solicitors Act to hear any application to strike a solicitor off the roll of solicitors, and in 1919 it acquired the actual power of striking off, until then exercised by the High Court. The civil engineers established an Institute in 1818. The architects formed their Institution in 1834. An Institution of mechanical engineers was set up in 1847. And the chemists obtained a Royal Institute in 1877 (Millerson 1964:121, 126; Manchester 1980:67).

Other groups were unashamedly concerned to protect the vested interests of their members. During the second half of the nineteenth century schoolteachers began to organize themselves in order to improve their status. The National Union of Elementary Teachers, the forerunner of the present-day National Union of Teachers, was created following the passage of the 1870 Education Act; it campaigned for better conditions of service for teachers and maintained a watching brief on educational developments, scoring some notable victories in the framing of the Education Act of 1902 (Tropp 1957:160–82). The British Medical Association, which originated in the 1830s, established a Parliamentary Bills Committee and was able to call upon the services of sympathetic MPs, often medical practioners themselves, in order to make its voice heard whenever medical matters were under discussion (Vaughan 1959:46, 53–5).

These groups were as concerned with the internal structure and discipline of their professions as with their status in the wider world. But others were preoccupied almost exclusively with the protection of common interests, whether in relation to Parliament and the government, or in relation to other groups, such as consumers. A Booksellers' Association, formed in 1848, attempted unsuccessfully to enforce a net book agreement; this object was eventually achieved by the Publishers' Association in 1895 (Wootton 1975:77). The 1880s saw the establishment of a National Federation of Property Owners, and in the following decade there was a flurry of activity within the retail trade, whose members were anxious to establish the principle of resale price maintenance. The establishment of the Employers' Parliamentary Council has already been noted. It was complemented by the foundation of the National Chamber of Trade in 1897, the Institute of Directors in 1903, and the Manufacturers' Association two years later.

Of equal significance was the mushrooming of philanthropic and 'worthy cause' groups: the Anti-Slavery Society in 1823; the Royal Society for the Prevention of Cruelty to Animals (1824); the anti-drink United Kingdom Alliance (1853); the Travelling Tax Abolition Committee (1877); the National Society for the Prevention of Cruelty to Children (1884); and literally scores of others. Some of these bodies, such as the Charity Organization Society, were not primarily political. But all of them were bound, by the very nature of their activities, to do business with the organs of central and local government. Towering above them, and upon whose success many nineteenth-century groups modelled themselves, was the Anti-Corn Law League. The League's judicious mixture of political activity, parliamentary action and public propaganda marked it out as both a lobby and an interest group, but also as much more besides. It must, on any reckoning, be considered the most successful pressure group of its age. It appealed to a broad cross-section of British society, encompassed the right mixture of radicalism and moderation necessary to achieve its objective, and played a political game without itself becoming a political party.

In appealing for the support of the largely unenfranchised working classes, the League succeeded where the Chartists failed. This is not the place to compare and contrast the two movements. Suffice it to say that the League offered the working classes 'jam today'; the abolition of the corn duty was bound to lead to a reduction in the price of bread, by a process of simple arithmetic which all could grasp. Chartism, by contrast, offered 'political reform today, leading (perhaps) to jam tomorrow'. The working classes of Victorian England were not particularly interested in political reform *per se*. They were not enraged by the absence of the right to vote, and the spectre of annual parliaments hardly excited them. They were concerned, as working-class people always have been concerned, with bread-and-butter issues: pay; conditions and hours of work; somewhere to live. The trade unions which they formed in the mid-nineteenth century were little more than glorified friendly societies, and the Trades Union Congress was, from the start, dedicated to working within the existing parliamentary structure to protect and extend trade-union rights. The trade unions themselves were non-political. But towards the very end of the century this political neutrality came under attack. One of the hallmarks of 'New Unionism' in the 1890s was the attempt by socialists to use the trade-union movement as a vehicle for the attainment of political objectives.

The trade unions, even the New Unions such as Havelock Wilson's National Sailors' and Firemen's Union, or Tom Mann's Dock, Wharf, Riverside and General Labourers' Union, were or became pressure groups. The Social-Democratic Federation and the Independent Labour Party – but not the Fabian Society – were political parties, whose aim was to fight elections and achieve parliamentary representation. The line is, admittedly, not easy to draw. Some trade unions, such as the miners and the railwaymen's unions, also sponsored MPs. The Labour Representation Committee (from 1906 the Labour Party) was, and was meant to be, the political arm of the trade-union movement. Some representative organizations – for example, the Association of University Teachers and the Police Federation (both founded in 1919) – have always tried to interest a few MPs in their work (Perkin 1969; Judge 1968). Others, such as the Federation of British Industries (formed in 1916) have never experienced any difficulty in attracting parliamentary support. But, while all have tried to influence the taking of decisions by central government, none sought to take over, or to *be*, the central government. Even the Trades Union Congress has never sought this particular role for itself.

But between the beginning of the First World War and the end of the Second a subtle change took place in the relationship between many of these groups and the departments of central government (Middlemas 1979). Partly, though not entirely, through the exigencies of war, some representative groups found themselves sucked into the machinery of government. In 1915 the government introduced compulsory arbitration to resolve industrial disputes during wartime; this, together with government control of certain industries, fostered the growth of industry-wide wage settlements. But the government had to pay a price for this wartime collectivism. Trade unions were not only given extensive and enhanced negotiating rights; they were accorded wide access to, and indeed made a part of, the decision-making machinery to be found within the Whitehall bureaucracy.

During the First World War this access was, in general, only for the purposes of consultation. But in the Second World War the trade-union movement shared with government the responsibility for policy-making in economic and social matters. Central government accepted the view that it must always, in its labour policies, carry with it the spokesmen of industry; a National Joint Advisory Council, representing the Trades Union Congress and the British Employers' Confederation, was established to achieve this end (Macdonald, 1976:121). The depression of the 1930s also played a part in this process. The Federation of British Industries had been given a royal charter in 1923. It had a central role in the deliberations of the Import Duties Advisory Committee, established in 1932 to make recommendations on tariff matters (Glynn and Oxborrow 1976:138). Partnerships of this sort carried over into the immediate post-war period, and were refined and extended as the nation grappled with the problems of reconstruction. The Labour government's 1947 Agriculture Act provided public funds, and statutory rights of consultation, for the National Farmers' Union. And even if rights of representation and consultation were not actually enshrined in statute law, governments, of whatever political colour, took ever greater care to consult widely before proceeding with legislative or administrative action. Wide-ranging parliamentary debates were no longer a substitute for extensive consultation with those most likely to be affected by government policy.

In his historical examination of theories of representation in British politics, Professor S. H. Beer has demonstrated how, in the eighteenth century, the 'Old Tory' view of the constitution, which saw the role of representing the community as a whole as primarily the monarch's, was replaced by the 'Old Whig' view of a 'balanced constitution', in which the monarch shared with Parliament the duty of protecting the public interest (Beer 1969:15). Rotten boroughs, bribery and corruption could all be justified if they secured the return to the House of Commons of high-minded individuals, of independent means, who could give their time to the dispassionate consideration of what the public interest was, and how best it might be advanced. In the course of the nineteenth century this Old Whig view was supplanted by Liberal Individualism, with its gradual insistence upon the very *personal* representation which Burke had condemned (Beer, 1969:17, 34).

Before the onset of universal manhood suffrage (1918) it could have been argued that since not all groups in society were or could be represented in Parliament, the government had a duty to consult outside Westminster. But democracy, when it came, was, like justice, blind. Now it was only by the merest chance that particular interests were represented in Parliament; so the need to consult beyond the legislature was therefore greater than ever. Of course there were those who hankered after a semi-mythical 'golden age'. In his textbook *How Britain Is Governed* (1933), Professor Ramsay Muir bewailed the growth of 'sundry forces . . . [organized] . . . to resist the power of the Government, or to bring pressure to bear upon it'. These 'organized interests', Muir insisted, were 'outside the recognised machinery of the Constitution' because they brought pressure to bear on the government, not through Parliament, but 'directly, thus turning themselves into new forces of control over the Government'. He castigated the associations of local authorities and condemned the fact that 'the real discussion' on the 1929 Derating and Local Government Bill had taken place outside Parliament, in conferences between the Minister of Health and the local authorities. He observed that the banks, finance houses and the Stock Exchange exerted great pressure upon the Treasury. And he noted that the Federation of British Industries was actually conceived as an instrument to influence government without reference to Westminster. All these developments, to say nothing of the rising power of the trade unions, Professor Muir found 'exceedingly dangerous' and frankly unconstitutional (Muir 1933:306–11).

A generation later echoes of these sentiments are still to be found in and beyond the academic community. Sir Harold Wilson's treatise on *The Governance of Britain* (1976) mentions neither pressure groups, lobbies nor interests. A major work on British government by Sir Max Beloff and Gillian Peele devotes but twelve pages to the subject (including occasional references), though it is clear from their own description of the workings of government that pressure groups exist at all levels and that if they did not exist they would have to be (and on occasion actually are) invented (Beloff and Peele 1980).

In fact, over the past twenty years or so the growth in the number of pressure groups has been little short of spectacular. The *Directory of Pressure Groups and Representative Associations* lists well over 600, ranging from the Society for the Preservation of Beers from the Wood (whose purpose is to obtain legal definition of draught beer as opposed to keg or top pressure beer) and the Duodecimal Society (pledged to resisting metrication and to the abolition of decimal currency), to the large umbrella organizations such as the Trades Union Congress and the Confederation of British Industry. In compiling this work of reference some 2,000 bodies were selected as potential entries. Of those groups for which a date of foundation is given, more than half were formed in the 1960s and 1970s (Shipley 1979).

The roots of this growth seem to lie in the changing social and economic condition of Great Britain following the Second World War. The expansion of educational opportunities has brought into existence a new middle class, concerned with its environment and well able to articulate demands and to organize group activity. At the same time the flowering of a consumer-orientated society, with higher standards and higher expectations, has prompted public concern with matters which have been but imperfectly monitored, if monitored at all, hitherto. The formation of the Consumers' Association, in 1957, was both a landmark and a signpost: consumer*ism* had arrived. Two years later the Campaign for Nuclear Disarmanent was established, signalling not merely a deepening public concern with the implications of the new atomic technology, but also the rediscovery of the old techniques of mass demonstration and 'direct action'. It is clear, too, that the late 1950s witnessed the beginnings of a great disenchantment with the ability of established political parties to grapple with a wide variety of social issues, particularly those which (like homosexual law reform) cut across party lines. Certainly, the growth in number and membership of pressure groups coincided with a dramatic fall (by over a third) in membership of the Conservative and Labour parties (Alderman 1978a:71). A great many people now believe that causes are better pursued through pressure groups than through political parties.

The twin motors of higher material expectations and greater public concern with social conditions were also responsible for the formation of the Child Poverty Action Group (1965) and the housing group Shelter (1966). Significantly, perhaps, both groups owed a great deal of their inspiration to Quakers, and their establishment was consciously linked with the great social reform movements of the nineteenth century (Bradley 7 Apr. 1980:2). They were led by young radicals, such as Frank Field and Des Wilson, who dispensed with discreet lobbying behind closed doors in favour of flamboyant public campaigns. The new medium of television was harnessed to great effect by men and women whose approach to pressure-group politics was entirely professional. The management of the 'peak' or 'umbrella' organizations had always been in the hands of paid professionals. During the 1960s and 1970s many other groups, notably in the fields of consumerism, social reform and environmentalism, also came under the direction of full-time salaried experts. A new industry had been called into being.

We are now in a better position to appreciate both the profundity and the superficiality of Arthur Bentley's revelations at the turn of the century. And we are also better equipped to know what pressure groups are and what they are not. Even by those who accept their role without question (whether or not they approve of it), there is still some reluctance to use the term 'pressure groups'. Professor Finer dislikes the term because (he says) 'pressure' implies that 'some kind of sanction will be applied if a demand is refused, and most groups, most of the time, simply make requests to put a case; they reason and they argue, but they do not threaten' (Finer 1966:3). This objection seems to be founded upon an imperfect understanding of what pressure groups do. Granted that many groups do have a sanction which they are at liberty to impose; yet many do not. 'Pressure' does not *always* imply 'sanction', but it does always imply the deliberate bringing to bear of 'power'. Sometimes this will indeed carry a threat of physical force or, more often, that violence will ensue if the demands of a pressure group are not met. But it may consist in nothing more than concerted action, a mass lobby of Parliament, for example, or a propaganda campaign. Some of the most successful pressure-group campaigns in British history (the anti-slavery movement and the movement for the abolition of the death penalty for murder spring to mind at once) had no sanction at all at their disposal. But the force they brought to bear proved overwhelming.

Dr G. K. Roberts defines a pressure group as 'an organized group which has as one of its purposes the exercise of influence (or "pressure") on political institutions, for the purpose of securing favourable decisions or preventing unfavourable ones' (Roberts 1971:173). It is clear from his subsequent discussion of this definition that he means 'political institutions' to encompass not merely legislators, but the executive and even, in the United States, the judiciary. It is also clear that he recognizes that though pressure groups are to be distinguished from political parties, 'some organizations are on the margin'. Yet he insists that a pressure group differs from an interest 'in so far as it is organized'.

This seems to me quite unnecessarily restrictive. Just as a nineteenth-century interest may have been organized or unorganized, so may a twentieth-century pressure group. Those individuals who come together as a pressure group share common aims and interests. Their opinions as to how these interests can best be advanced may well vary a great deal. Sometimes the variations are so great that a split occurs, formally or informally: one thinks of the 'physical force' and 'moral force' Chartists, or the Campaign for Nuclear Disarmament and the more militant Committee of One Hundred. A pressure group itself, however, need not have any formal structure. Very often local amenity groups are of this sort: parents asking for a school-crossing patrol; local residents anxious to prevent atmospheric pollution from a nearby factory, or to stamp out vandalism on a housing estate, or to prevent dangerous loads from being carried by road through populated areas (*The Times*, 5 Nov. 1981:2). Such associations of people with common objectives are hardly 'interests'.

But we should beware of supposing that unorganized pressure groups exist only at local level, or only among cause groups. Some examples of unorganized pressure groups are given in Chapter 2. Here we must note that by far the largest and most powerful unorganized pressure group in Britain is, and has for the past 200 years or more been, 'the City' – the merchant banks, finance houses, bill brokers, bullion traders, stockbrokers and insurance companies whose offices are crowded into the square mile of the City of London. The life-style, purposes and *modi operandi* of the City fulfil all the criteria of Dr Roberts' definition of a pressure group. The City is a 'peak' conglomerate, containing within itself a number of formal groupings, and with the Bank of England as its mouthpiece. Yet it possesses no formal organization of its own (Ferris 1960:14–15).

But just as pressure groups are not, in general, political parties (for they do not aim to take over the government of the country) so they are not to be found among the formal agencies or organs of government. They may well have official, even statutory roles to fulfil within a particular government department or governmental organization. And it is equally true that government departments put pressure upon each other, on the Cabinet and on Parliament, and on groups wholly outside the government. There are those observers of political systems in western societies who regard government departments or agencies *as* pressure groups, to be distinguished from other pressure groups only by virtue of their being 'official'. To understand how such a view can be held we must return to Bentley. He saw 'all phenomena of government' as 'phenomena of groups pressing one another' (Bentley 1967:269). The state of government was thus the existing balance of competing groups. Bentley's disciple Earl Latham asserted that public policy was 'a balance which the contending factions of groups constantly strive to weight in their favor' (E. Latham 1965:36). So far as Latham is concerned, the 'official' groups differ from the 'unofficial' only by virtue of their ability 'to exercise against all groups and individuals certain powers which they ["all groups and individuals"] may not exercise' against the former (E. Latham 1965:35). Government, in this model, is just one group among many.

Now there may well be very good grounds for regarding the operation of the policy process in this light. Of course government departments exert pressure on each other, and of course they have their own aims which they pursue through a variety of official and unofficial channels. The policy outcomes of British central government are as much the product of inter- and intra-departmental conflicts as of pressures from outside. Until she became a Cabinet minister in 1964 the Labour politician Barbara Castle thought that Cabinets actually decided on policies to be pursued, on the basis of political priorities. Experience taught her differently: 'I suddenly found I wasn't in a political caucus at all. I was faced by departmental enemies' (Castle 1973). The 'group' theory of politics may therefore be well-grounded so far as policy formation is concerned. But to regard an entire *system of government* in this light is to descend to the level of a meaningless generality. Odegard, Bentley's editor, rightly observes that the term 'interest group' would then become synonymous 'not merely with politics but with human life itself' (Odegard 1958:695).

Academic trenches have been well and truly dug around this argument. David Truman refined and dilated upon Bentley in his own book, *The Governmental Process*, first published in 1951. 'The behaviors that constitute the process of government', Truman argued, 'cannot be adequately understood apart from the groups . . . which are operative at any point in time' (Truman 1971:502). Bentley, indeed, had implicitly denied the importance of the individual in the process of government (Bentley 1967:224–5). In Britain Professor Bernard Crick has labelled Bentley as obscurantist and lacking in historical discipline (Crick 1959:128). But we should remember that Bentley was merely 'fashioning a tool' for others to use in empirical studies of government. Because a political party may, at one time or another, exhibit many of the characteristics of a pressure group, and may even have developed from a collection of such groups, does not mean that it is itself a pressure group. Similarly, because a government department may, at any given moment, behave like a pressure group does not mean that we would be justified in calling it a pressure group. In the British context, at any rate, to do so is to confuse several quite distinct elements in the matrix of government.

Just as pressure groups do not aim to take over the government of the country, so they are not coterminous with the machinery of government. Nor, it must be added, is the purpose of a pressure group always to influence *government*, if by that word we mean the organs of government narrowly defined–i.e. Parliament, the Cabinet, the civil service, the judiciary. The aim of a pressure group may be simply to influence public opinion, or just a special subsection of the population. Many ethical and moral groups are of this type. For the purpose of understanding the role of pressure groups, we may define them as those units, organized or not, of the democratic process which have a set purpose or a set of purposes, but which are nonetheless neither political parties nor formal agencies of government. They have evolved, historically, as a form of functional representation made necessary by the limitations of or defects within other organs of British government: principally, the atrophy of traditional methods of representation of views and accountability; the decline of popular faith in the parliamentary process; the growth in power of the civil service; and the inability or unwillingness of political parties to deal with particularly sensitive issues. They fulfil needs which are nowhere else serviced. They are an integral part of the political, parliamentary and governmental process in this country. They are as much a part of the machinery of the constitution as the monarch Herself.

Chapter two
ANATOMY

The classification of pressure groups has become a veritable cottage industry among political scientists. The late Professor Frank Stacey distinguished two major types of pressure group: 'interest' groups and 'ideas' groups (Stacey 1968:319–20). The first he subdivided into producer groups (such as the Confederation of British Industry) and consumer groups (such as the Automobile Association). By an 'ideas' group he meant one whose members do not stand to benefit materially from the end which they pursue. But having categorized pressure groups in terms of self-interest, or the lack of it, he then added a third category, 'the *ad hoc* committee' which disappears when its end has been achieved.

Curiously, Stacey did not consider it worthwhile to differentiate *ad hoc* interest groups from *ad hoc* ideas groups, and he readily admitted that it was difficult to define '*ad hoc*' in temporal terms (Stacey 1968:321). He also conceded that there was in reality no clear-cut division between interest groups and ideas groups. It is easy to see why. Many ideas groups seek to propagate views which, incidentally, benefit their own members. Adherents of the Campaign for Nuclear Disarmament argue that their concern for their own perceived well-being, in the face of the proliferation of nuclear weapons, is an element in their group motivation; they are an ideas group with a great deal of self-interest. Similarly, there are many groups which Stacey would have classified as interest groups, but which actually propagate ideas which (so they claim) are for the benefit of the general population. In the summer of 1978, when it was widely expected that a general election would be called in the autumn, the Campaign Against Building Industry Nationalisation – 'CABIN' – a consortium of building and civil engineering employers, spent a great deal of money distributing circulars attacking the Labour Party's plans to take large sections of the building industry into public ownership and control (*Sunday Times*, 9 July 1978:3). One of CABIN's arguments was that nationalization of the building industry would push up building costs, and that this was against the national interest. In that case, was CABIN an interest group or an ideas group? Stacey would no doubt have said that it was an *ad hoc* committee, and left it at that!

We may say that Stacey's classification is based upon supposed motivation, grounded perhaps in the belief that an understanding of motives will deepen our understanding of the role of pressure groups within the overall system of government Stacey set out to describe. But, even supposing that were so, so many are the exceptions to the classification, and so frequent are the cases of overlap between different groups or sub-groups, that in the end one is left with little more than the remnants of an intellectual exercise, too academic to be of much practical value.

Professor Finer takes an altogether more pragmatic view, by classifying lobbies on socio-economic lines (Finer 1966:8–18). First come industrial and commercial groups, or the 'business' lobby, at the head of which stand the Confederation of British Industry, the Institute of Directors and the Association of British Chambers of Commerce. Next, and to some extent in juxtaposition to the first, Finer identifies the 'Labour' lobby (not the 'Labour Party' lobby), consisting of trade unions large and small, and the Trades Union Congress. The Co-operative movement Finer puts into a separate category of its own. Fourth, Finer lists the professions. Then come a medley of 'civic groups', ranging from the National Council of Social Service to the Hansard Society for Parliamentary Government; and following these Finer lists a number of bodies which cater for 'special social categories' of the population, such as the disabled, the aged, motorists, and so on. Religious bodies form a seventh and quite separate category, and finally Finer groups together a number of educational, cultural and recreational groups.

As with Stacey's classification, one must ask whether Finer's typology actually contributes towards an understanding of the impact of pressure groups – or even 'lobbies' – on the mechanism of government. Even as an aid to an understanding of what lobbies are, the typology is of limited value. For example, Finer excludes from the business lobby the institutions of the City of London, whose discreet opinions weigh heavily on the minds of the Treasury mandarins. He deliberately separates out the professions from the 'Labour' lobby; but one of the 'professional' organizations he singles out for special treatment, the National and Local Government

Officers' Association, affiliated to the Trades Union Congress between the appearance of the first and second editions of his book, and a number of teaching organizations, such as the National Union of Teachers and the Association of University Teachers, are now also TUC-affiliated. Other professional bodies, such as the British Medical Association, the Inland Revenue Staff Federation, and the Royal College of Nursing, behave very much as labour lobbies, and the various civil service societies and associations are out-and-out trade unions.

Finer himself declares that 'there is no sanctity' about his classi-ication, and he admits that some of his categories 'tend to overlap' Finer 1966:18). For it is precisely the multi-functional nature of nodern British pressure groups which frustrates categorization ılong socio-economic lines. Either the categories are too large to be ıf much value to the student of British government; or they are too mall for any valid conclusions to be drawn from their component ıarts about each category as a whole. Allen Potter, who pioneered ıe field of British pressure-group typology, has claimed to identify venty-four different types of organized interests (Potter 1961:Chs. and 6). This is fine as a guidebook and a work of reference. But it ınnot, by itself, take us much further than Finer does in grasping ıe essentials of pressure groups as institutions of government; it is a irectory rather than an explanation.

A yet more complex typology has been constructed by Professor Vootton, a former British civil servant and university don who now eaches at Tufts University, Massachusetts. Wootton's typology is ased both on the degree of political specialization of each group, and n the degree of the group's openness of membership or recruit-ıent. From these twin measurements he derives a 'matrix' of four ells: 'representative' groups which have a given or closed mem-ıership and a high degree of political involvement, such as the Welsh Language Society and the Trades Union Congress; 'oper-ıtional' groups, which have a closed membership but 'low' political nvolvement (the Welsh League of Youth and the National Union of Railwaymen are given as examples); 'expressive' groups with a low political involvement but an open membership, such as the National Trust and the Workers' Educational Association; and 'propagation-al' groups with an open membership but a well-developed sense of political initiative, such as the Child Poverty Action Group, Shelter, and the National Council for Civil Liberties (Wootton 1978:20).

As an exercise in political science methodology Professor Woot-ton's matrix is certainly fascinating. But it is hard to discern its practical application. The placing of a particular group in a particular cell of the matrix is, as the Professor himself admits, based on 'rough and challengeable judgments . . . mainly because we lack sufficient knowledge of the functional mix (politics/other-than-politics) in each instance, which is in principle discoverable' (Wootton 1978:19). Even the choice of names for the four groups is admitted to be arbitrary. More worrying, however, is the suspicion that Professor Wootton's concept of what is 'political' is dangerously narrow; he may mean 'party political', but this is far from clear. No matter. The bulk of Professor Wootton's book is a compendium of blow-by-blow accounts of activities undertaken by the various groups he describes. As such – and ignoring the typology – it is a mine of information and a tribute to his breadth of knowledge of the activities in which all manner of British pressure groups are engaged.

We should also note, for the sake of completeness, that some typologies have been designed with specific topics in mind. In her examination of the role of pressure groups in relation to the permissive society, Bridget Pym declares that 'the most important dividing line is between groups that are politically acceptable and groups that are not'. The latter are not politically acceptable 'because they propagandize for unpopular causes or minority interests, or because they are judged unrepresentative of those they claim to speak for'; the former are 'readily and regularly admitted to consultations with government departments' (Pym 1974:19).

Now this differentiation begs a multitude of questions. For instance, the Lord's Day Observance Society certainly propagandizes for a minority interest; but it is far from being politically unacceptable. The Royal Society for the Prevention of Cruelty to Animals is readily and regularly admitted to consultations with government departments; but some of its policies, such as its opposition to the slaughter of food animals without prior stunning, have never found widespread favour in political circles. Pym's definition is certainly more than adequate to cover the subject-matter of her book: issues such as abortion law reform, the abolition of hanging, homosexual law reform, divorce law reform. It is very helpful to be able to explain and explore these topics in terms of 'institutionalized groups', such as the Police Federation, the Prison Officers' Association, the Catholic Women's League and the British Medical Association, and 'radical groups', like the Marriage Law Reform Society, the Abortion Law Reform Association, and the Homosexual Law Reform Society (Pym 1974:55–64). But such a typology, admittedly useful as an aid to our understanding of certain historical processes, has no wider applicability. If we wished to adopt this approach to help in a more general understanding of the impact of pressure groups on British government, we should have to construct a different typology for each type of issue we came across.

Most classifications of pressure groups are derived from allegedly common characteristics within the groups themselves. Since many pressure groups share certain features, no such compartmentalization can ever be watertight. Kimber and Richardson deliberately – and rightly – warn of the dangers inherent in categorization (Kimber and Richardson, 1974(a):12). The greatest stumbling-block, however, is the fact that politics is a dynamic activity. A pressure group formed for one purpose may in time come to fulfil other purposes also. The Automobile Association began its life in 1905 as an organization of motorists intent on thwarting police speed-traps on the Brighton road; it is now consulted by the Department of Transport on a wide variety of motoring matters, and in relation to the compulsory wearing of seat belts (which it favours) has adopted a position to which many motorists object. This example demonstrates how a single pressure group may, over the course of time, move from one role to another. It may, indeed, change out of all recognition. The Shipping Federation was founded in 1890 as an unashamed strike-breaking and blackleg-supplying organization; today it is a highly respected body representative of shipowners on all matters connected with maritime affairs.

Thus any categorization, however complex and refined, is rooted in time and may soon become hopelessly out of date. Moreover, there is a danger that such categorization will impute to pressure groups a unity of purpose which is wholly artificial, or a set of characteristics which is not in fact shared by all groups in a particular category. This is no help to an understanding of pressure groups; it merely deepens the mists which surround them and leads the political scientist to fashion monuments to the glory of misplaced academic endeavour.

The notion of permanency, espoused by Stacey, is a case in point. Roberts has adopted this approach, and regards the question of permanency as a real yardstick by which pressure groups may be measured (Roberts 1970:89–90). An *ad hoc* group, according to Dr Roberts, is one which has a single purpose capable of complete satisfaction by political action. Now it is perfectly true that examples of such groups may easily be found. At local level, indeed, such groups are commonplace, for their aims are limited (and often negative) and, unless part of a wider, national body, they usually lack the resources to achieve permanency, which they probably do not desire anyway. The Wing Airport Resistance Association ('WARA'), formed for a finite and highly specific purpose, is a good example of this type of group. It arose out of the Labour government's decision, in 1968, to appoint the Roskill Commission to investigate possible sitings for London's third airport (Kimber and Richardson, 1974(b):168–9). Four sites were considered; the aim of WARA was to make certain that the government's choice did not fall upon Cublington, an allegedly picturesque village in north Buckinghamshire. WARA lost the first round in this battle, for in spite of a concentrated and highly professional publicity campaign, and the retention of a distinguished lawyer to present its case, the Roskill Commission recommended Cublington to the government. But the recommendation was never carried out. WARA purchased for itself the advice of professional public relations experts; was supported by Buckinghamshire County Council and by many Members of Parliament; and cleverly exploited differences of opinion within the Roskill Commission, voiced by Professor Colin Buchanan. In 1971 the Conservative government, ignoring Roskill, chose the bird-infested marshes of Essex known as Foulness. Only the naturalists protested (Flewin 1975:73–81).

Virtually every town and village in the country can boast a pressure group of this sort, formed for a single purpose and which disappears when that purpose is achieved: groups to prevent factory development; to obtain a by-pass, or to prevent one being built; to close a road to heavy traffic; to preserve some local amenity; to promote recreational facilities, such as the building of a swimming-pool; to prevent the establishment or continuation of a controversial form of entertainment, such as a circus or a sex-shop. But most such groups are directed against local rather than against national government. WARA was a spectacular oddity: a local group fighting a national issue.

At national level examples of such 'finite' groups are much rarer. The Anti-Corn Law League, which dissolved itself once the Corn Laws had been repealed, in 1846, is the most famous example. The Equal Pay Campaign Committee, formed in order to achieve equal rates of pay for male and female employees in the public service, was dissolved in 1956 when the Conservative government agreed to the phased introduction of equal pay (Potter 1957:49–64). But such examples are exceptions to the rule. At national level most pressure-group campaigns are never decisively won or lost. Positions won have to be defended and, especially when a prospect exists of a decision of central government being reversed after a general election, the vanquished can live on in the hope of victory next time. The National Campaign for the Abolition of Capital Punishment has never achieved its avowed objective. It achieved a partial success when the Homicide Act of 1957 distinguished between capital and non-capital murder; and in 1969 Parliament voted to continue indefinitely the suspension of the death penalty for murder, enacted in 1965. But the death penalty remains on the statute book (for the offence of treason), and a gallows is kept in working order at Wandsworth prison. From time to time since 1969 supporters of hanging have forced the issue upon the attention of MPs, so that the anti-capital punishment lobby must be ever-vigilant, and cannot afford to rest on its laurels.

There is another aspect to this matter. Local pressure groups which lack formal structure dissolve themselves automatically as soon as a stated goal has been reached. But once a group becomes organized, and particularly once it has acquired a bureaucratic infrastructure, its dissolution is difficult. For once an organization is formed, those who participate in it, and who derive status and influence from being associated with it, are only too anxious that it should remain in being. The Labour Representation Committee, formed on the initiative of the Trades Union Congress in 1899 to reverse, by legislation, the hostile trend of judge-made law affecting trade unions, was not dissolved once the Trade Disputes Act had been passed in 1906. The Popular Television Association, established in 1953 to press for the introduction of commercial television in Britain, achieved its objective when Parliament passed the Television Act in 1954, setting up the Independent Television Authority (H. H. Wilson 1961). In 1961, however, the Association was resurrected, under the name of the National Broadcasting Development Committee, to secure the introduction of commercial radio (achieved with the passage of the Broadcasting Act, 1972) and a second commercial television channel (which began operating in 1982)

Dr Roberts argues that the Campaign for Nuclear Disarmament is an *ad hoc* group, because its purposes would be fulfilled if Britain gave up nuclear weapons. In the view of the present author unilateral nuclear disarmament by Britain would be seen by many within the Campaign as the first step in a world-wide movement; the Campaign would not be wound up, but would broaden out, perhaps with a change of title, and would become internationally-orientated. We might also note that even WARA, which appears on the surface a perfect example of a successful *ad hoc* group, possessed a prehistory. Wing is sixteen miles from Silverton, in Northamptonshire, which had at one stage been considered as a possible airport site. A local barrister had formed the Silverton Airport Resistance Association ('SARA'), and it was this association which, 'with very little change of personnel', became WARA (Madgwick 1976:289). Although, therefore, Dr Roberts's notion of permanency certainly does have some validity, it seems too limited to be of much practical general application. Interesting as theory, it breaks down when applied to the practicalities of British government.

Other categorizations are no less flawed. Some observers have attempted to distinguish between promotional and defensive groups, arguing that promotional groups seek to persuade government or Parliament to initiate some reform or to embark on some course of action, while defensive groups seek to prevent others from undoing what has already been done. An example of the former would be the Abortion Law Reform Association, which in 1966 mounted a parliamentary and public campaign to widen considerably the grounds upon which a registered medical practitioner might perform an abortion. The Association obtained the support of an all-party group of MPs and – more important – the benevolent neutrality of the Labour government, which assisted in the drafting of a Bill and gave parliamentary time to ensure that it would not be 'talked out'. In 1967 the Abortion Act came into force. But the activities of the Association inevitably gave rise to opposition, particularly from the Roman Catholic Church. A Society for the Protection of Unborn Children was established, and was able to mobilise the support of most Roman Catholic MPs. The Society was unable to prevent the passage of the 1967 legislation, but since then has launched several unsuccessful assaults upon the Act, and has been active at the hustings in pressing its views upon electors. In 1967 the Abortion Law Reform Association was clearly a promotional group, and the Society a defensive one. A decade or so later the roles were reversed. In 1980 a bitter struggle took place when the Society obtained the support of the Conservative MP John Corrie and, in a parliamentary climate radically different from that of 1967, came within an ace of substantially repealing the 1967 Act.

So, although the notions of promotion and defence have some relevance, they are rooted in time. More seriously, such an analysis, though it can be applied fairly easily to 'single cause' groups, fails to make an impact when applied to the much larger pressure organizations, whose fields of activity will inevitably lead them to wage both offensive and defensive campaigns. In addition, there are a great many pressure groups which stubbornly refuse to fit into either category. The Stop the Seventy Tour Committee took literally the military maxim that the best form of defence is attack. It was formed in August 1969 to prevent a South African cricket tour of Britain planned for the following year from taking place. Its methods were frankly physical and disruptive, and it flexed its muscles by playing havoc with the tour of Britain which the South African Springboks rugby-football team made in the winter of 1969–70. So violent did some of these fixtures become that the Home Secretary prevailed upon the British cricket authorities to cancel the cricket tour (this campaign is more fully treated in Chapter 5).

The promotional/defensive dichotomy is of no relevance to an understanding of how such a group works. But when one comes to examine the tactics of groups whose purpose is to maintain a watching brief over a whole range of public issues, one is forced to conclude that their repertoire must, of necessity, include both promotional and defensive measures. This is palpably obvious in the case of the great umbrella organizations. Following the passage of the 1971 Industrial Relations Act, the Trades Union Congress launched a massive campaign to defend, in defiance of the Act, what it regarded as inalienable trade-union rights. At the same time it promoted the concept of worker-directors, eventually endorsed in the Bullock Report of 1977. Meanwhile, the Confederation of British Industry was launching a campaign against official 'blacklisting' of firms which ignored the Labour government's pay guidelines. In 1981 the Confederation launched an equally vigorous campaign to try to persuade the Conservative administration to abolish the employers' National Insurance surcharge. In the world of pressure politics attack is indeed often the best form of defence. The National Viewers' and Listeners' Association was launched in 1965 to rid television and radio of what its supporters considered the harmful portrayal of sex and violence in these media (Tracey and Morrison 1979:47). It realized, however, that it would need to change the law to achieve this, and has waged a number of parliamentary campaigns to this end. In 1978 it sponsored a campaign entitled 'ABUSE' (Action to Ban Sexual Exploitation of Children), the object of which was to persuade a sceptical Parliament to agree to legislation against child pornography. A willing and interested MP, Mr Cyril Townsend, was found to promote a Bill, which was passed into law with a great deal of publicity outside Westminster but with dangerously little parliamentary debate (McCarthy and Moodie 1981).

Clearly, no categorization or typology of pressure groups is going to be wholly satisfactory or completely free from defect. Of those examined so far, some possess a limited general applicability. None, however, are of much assistance in understanding how pressure groups interact with government, less still what part they play in the process of government. In modern British society power – the ability to achieve at acceptable cost the aims one sets for oneself – is dependent upon the sanctions that one has at one's disposal and which one is able to apply. *Where* one applies them – in Whitehall, at Westminster, during elections, through the media, via a strike – is a different matter (though obviously related), and will be considered in later chapters. Here my concern is with the *availability* of sanctions, and the range of them at a group's disposal. A typology of pressure groups along these lines, though not without shortcomings, seems the most useful way of understanding their impact upon the society in which we live.

But a categorization needs also to take some account of the client group on whose behalf the sanction is being applied. The most widely accepted categorization along these lines (and one in respect of which the present author can claim no originality whatsoever) relies on a distinction between those groups which represent a section of the community, or which campaign on behalf of such a section, and those which champion a cause or set of causes, a belief or dogma, not associated with the vested interests of any particular section of the community. This type of approach has been adopted (albeit not in the precise form just stated) by J. D. Stewart (Stewart 1957:25) and Dr R. M. Punnett (Punnett 1976:136–9). Other writers, such as Dr Roberts (Roberts, 1970:91) have appeared to follow it, or at least to have acknowledged its usefulness, though their interpretation of 'sectional' and 'cause' clearly differs from my own. W. N. Coxall, for example, argues that the Child Poverty Action Group is a 'cause' or 'attitude' group (Coxall 1981:11). Yet it acts on behalf of a sectional interest, the infant poor, and in June 1976 its director carried out one of the most successful coups in the annals of British pressure-group history by obtaining and printing Cabinet minutes concerning the government's child-benefit scheme; the government was shown to have acted dishonestly in postponing the introduction of the scheme, which was implemented in 1977 (Herbert 1978). Similarly, the mental health charities 'MIND' and 'MENCAP' advance the special interests of the mentally handicapped, and played a prominent part in the public discussion and passage of the government's Bill to reform the mental health laws, in 1981–82 (*The Times*, 12 Nov. 1981:5; 14 Jan. 1982:24).

All sectional groups are able to apply a sanction, though its strength will naturally vary as between one sectional group and another. A cause group *may* be able to impose a strong sanction. The 'Greenpeace' conservation group, for example, has been known to physically interpose itself between whaling ships and the whales it seeks to protect. In general, however, the ability of cause groups to apply a sanction varies from very weak to moderate; that of sectional groups from moderate to very strong. We must now examine in more detail examples of groups in each category.

Trade unions and trade associations stand out as sectional groups with strong coercive powers. The Trades Union Congress is the major group representing organized labour in Great Britain; over 11 million workers belong to unions which are affiliated to it, and over 100 unions send delegates to its annual conferences. The formal powers of the TUC, and of its General Secretary, are very limited. The TUC cannot intervene in the internal affairs of member unions, neither can it negotiate agreements which bind member unions, nor does it represent all working people in Britain. It may expel a union, and in September 1971 it resolved to use this power against all unions which persisted in registering under the new Industrial Relations Act; 20 unions, with a total membership of 370,000, including the Health Service Employees, the Bank Employees and the National Union of Seamen, were expelled thereby.

But expulsion is a rather blunt instrument, for a union, once expelled, is virtually beyond the TUC's persuasive reach. The strength of the TUC derives from the fact that its membership includes trade unions with real industrial muscle (such as the Mineworkers, the Railwaymen, and the Transport and General Workers' Union), and that its opinions are respected by most trade unionists, even if they are not always heeded. The TUC is represented on a wide range of public bodies and can generally expect to be consulted on many aspects of government policy involving the regulation of labour. It elects six representatives to the Council of the National Economic Development Office; is formally represented on the Manpower Services Commission, the Health and Safety Commission, and the Arbitration and Conciliation Service; and appoints members to a great many agencies or adjuncts of government, such as the Coal Consumers' Council, the Export Credit Guarantee Advisory Council, and the Metrication Board (Richardson and Jordan 1979:50). In choosing which persons to select for each of the appointments within its gift, the TUC naturally has regard to the expertise at its disposal. This means that senior officials of member unions can look forward to nomination, as TUC representatives, to bodies of particular interest to their members; for example, the TUC has the right to nominate one member of the Council (governing body) of Brunel University; in 1981 its nominee was the General Secretary of the Association of University Teachers.

It is partly through the patronage at its disposal that the TUC enjoys the loyalty of its member unions. Through membership of the Congress, even relatively small unions acquire access to decision-making processes which might otherwise be denied to them. This can compensate for lack of industrial muscle. Unions which are not particularly strong by themselves acquire strength through TUC membership. For by refusing to co-operate with government (as in 1971) the TUC is in a position to effectively frustrate government policy. But it can also be a powerful ally. In April 1976 the Labour Chancellor of the Exchequer proposed that increases in personal tax allowances should be conditional on the TUC accepting Phase Two of the government's incomes policy, which limited pay increases to about 3 per cent from July. This agreement was reached in May. Thus did the TUC come to play a major part in government handling of the nation's financial affairs.

It is commonplace to regard the Confederation of British Industry as the employers' equivalent of the TUC. But in terms of pressure-group status such a comparison is misleading. The CBI is, as its name states, a *confederation*. It was formed in 1965 through a merger between three much older bodies, the National Association of British Manufacturers, the British Employers' Confederation, and the Federation of British Industries. Through membership of the CBI, 11,000 or so companies can have a voice in the formulation of policy which, they may be sure, will reach the ears and eyes of the government and Parliament. The CBI primarily represents private manufacturing industry. Most of its members are in the private manufacturing sector, though the leading banks, some insurance companies, and even some nationalized industries have become members too. It does not represent the retail trade, which is organized through the Retail Consortium, and from time to time there have been rumblings of discontent from the largest and smallest of its members. At the end of the 1960s there was a double revolt. On the one hand many small firms seceded to form the Small Business Association (now the Association of Independent Businesses). On the other, there was a split between heads of large private companies, who wished the CBI to press for a reduction in the size of the public sector, and the chairmen of nationalized industries, who were opposed to the sale of parts of the public sector back into private hands. In 1976 the nationalized industries formed a ginger-group, known as the Group of Twenty-One, within the CBI (Coxall 1981:79–80).

The CBI has a sanction it can impose against rebellious members, though the sanction is not a particularly potent one. Under the provisions of paragraph 13 of the Confederation's bye-laws, a member company may be required to 'withdraw' at any time; but this has never happened, and it is most unlikely that it ever would happen. The disciplining of member companies is not the CBI's style, and would involve absolutely no material penalty. However, the CBI is in a position, directly and indirectly, to impose sanctions against the government. Its budget runs into several millions of pounds annually, and it therefore has the resources, to say nothing of the expertise, to engage in publicity and research, and to challenge government policy. Like the TUC, it has the right of representation on many public bodies, including the National Economic Development Office. Because of the industrial wealth it represents, both Labour and Conservative administrations have felt its agreement highly desirable in many areas of policy.

When this agreement is not forthcoming, trouble can result. In 1978, in an attempt to enforce upon private industry a non-statutory incomes policy, the Labour government declared that it would not award contracts to private firms which 'broke' its pay guidelines, and that such contracts as it did award would contain clauses obliging companies and their sub-contractors to adhere to the guidelines. Sir John Methven, the CBI's Director-General, threatened that the Confederation's General Council would recommend member companies to strike the proposed clauses from government contracts. Meanwhile, the CBI's Scottish Council asked its 1,200 member companies to 'black' all new government business, and Methven himself hinted that the CBI would bring the government before the Restrictive Practices Court. Many firms did in fact refuse to sign the new forms of contract. Faced with such intransigence the government gave ground, by agreeing to relax the responsibilities of contractors for sub-contractors, to an appeals procedure against government cancellation of contracts, and to the limitation of the controversial clauses to one round of pay negotiations (*The Times*, 13 Feb. 1978:1; 3 Mar. 1978:19).

This episode certainly showed the CBI at its most forceful. Yet it was not the first time that an industrial trade association had successfully frustrated government policy. In 1950 the British Iron and Steel Federation engaged in a policy of deliberate obstruction of the

Labour government's plans (sanctioned by Parliament) to nationalize the iron and steel industry. The Federation claimed that because Labour had obtained fewer seats in the general election of 1950 than it had had following the election of 1945, and because Labour had been returned to office in 1950 with less than 50 per cent of the votes cast, it had no mandate or moral right to proceed with the implementation of the nationalization Act. The policy of non-co-operation delayed effective implementation of the Act until the general election of 1951, when the Conservatives were returned to power with, as it happened, more seats than Labour but fewer votes. No further steps were taken to implement the Act and in 1953 it was repealed.

Of course not all industrial and commercial associations are in a position to impose sanctions with such devastating effectiveness. But we must remember that in a mixed economy any government depends on co-operation with the leaders of big business and is well advised to listen to what these leaders have to say. The precise nature of this relationship will be discussed later on. Here we must note that the major business groups generally find no difficulty in gaining access to the decision-making areas of government, and that in some areas their participation is vital, in part because, like the British Insurance Association or the Building Societies' Association, they control vast financial resources; their policies are able to influence the money markets, the value of sterling and, ultimately, the national balance of payments. Such influence is just as potent as the ability of certain trade unions to turn off the nation's gas and oil supplies, extinguish its electric lights, or bring train services to a halt.

There is a further body of sectional pressure groups to be considered: the numerous professional associations, some of which, like the Law Society, the Institute of Chartered Accountants, the Royal Institution of British Architects and the Royal Institution of Chartered Surveyors, actually conduct qualifying examinations for entry into the professions they represent. These are the twentieth-century equivalents of the medieval guilds. The professions they represent could not function without them. The Law Society, for example, controls all the examinations which solicitors in England and Wales must pass in order to qualify. It also administers the legal aid scheme, advises solicitors on professional ethics, and deals with complaints against solicitors. It is a jealous guardian of solicitors' rights, including the much-criticized monopoly of solicitors to engage in house conveyancing. In 1978 the Society instituted a prosecution against Mr Francis Whatsisname, the 'honorary conveyancer' of the Property Transfer Association, which offered 'cut-price' house conveyancing; the statutory privileges enshrined in the Solicitors Act were upheld, and Mr Whatsisname was fined £150 plus costs (*The Times*, 21 Jan. 1978:3). Clearly, the Law Society possesses a monopoly, sanctioned by Parliament. It would be unthinkable for any government to contemplate reforms in the legal system without taking the views of the Society into account – quite apart from the fact that both solicitors and barristers are well represented in Parliament. The Society does not need to impose a sanction; its 'negotiating' rights with the government are gilt-edged.

There are not many professional bodies whose powers are so extensive. Although membership of a major accounting body is one of the most widely recognized business qualifications, one does not have to be a qualified accountant to engage in business. Moreover, there are no less than six major associations of accountants in the United Kingdom: the Institute of Chartered Accountants in England and Wales; similar Institutes in Scotland and in Ireland; the Institute of Cost and Management Accountants; the Association of Certified Accountants; and the Institute of Public Finance and Accountancy. All are incorporated by Royal Charter, and each has its particular sphere of influence; all award accounting qualifications. Nonetheless, the prestige which these bodies enjoy is such that on matters involving, for example, company law, their representations will invariably be sought after, and will always be listened to.

The same is broadly true of other professional associations. Although membership of the British Insurance Brokers' Association is not an essential prerequisite to practising as an insurance broker, the Insurance Brokers Registration Act (1981) provides that anyone who calls himself an insurance broker must meet clearly defined standards of conduct and prove that he has the necessary professional expertise. The high standards demanded by the Association of its members, coupled with the requirements of the Act, mean that to all intents and purposes the Association is *the* trade association of the insurance-broking industry. Governments will always consult it on matters pertaining to this industry.

The concentration of expertise to be found in, say, the British Medical Association, or the British Dental Association, or the Royal Colleges of Physicians, of Surgeons, of General Practitioners or of Veterinary Surgeons, is such that not only is their complete access to government assured, but their active participation in areas of government within their purview is essential. All these Royal Colleges and medical Associations are, for instance, named in the 1971 Misuse of Drugs Act as having the right to nominate persons to tribunals and advisory bodies constituted under the Act. Were they to decide that the Act needed modification, their representations would have to be taken seriously, for governments know that without their co-operation parts of the Act would be unworkable. We might also recall, in this connection, that the British Medical Association has, on several occasions, sought to pressurise governments by threatening the withdrawal of its members' services. In 1946 it unsuccessfully attempted to cajole Parliament and the government into amending the National Health Service Act by declaring that its members would boycott the National Health Service unless its demands were met. In 1956 it made a similar threat in order to secure an interim pay award, and in 1965 the same type of threat secured a much-enhanced contract of service for National Health Service doctors.

But as one surveys the spectrum of professional groups, one moves from those with strong or very strong sanctions to those whose ability to influence decisions is frankly much weaker. The International Professional Security Association, which claims to be the leading British security organization, has 25,000 members and 15 regional councils in the United Kingdom. But although it has its own code of conduct, it has no control over non-members, and no means of restricting entry into the security business by 'cowboy' operators and 'fly-by-night' companies. This, in turn, means that its ability to 'represent' the British security industry is inevitably circumscribed, and that the sanctions it may deploy, either against security firms or (should it so wish) against the government, are very few (*The Times*, 23 Apr. 1982:6).

Some of the weaker sectional groups do nevertheless have powers of discipline over their own members, and such authority is sometimes upheld in the courts. The British Boxing Board of Control, an unincorporated non-statutory body, has wide powers to issue or to refuse licences to boxing managers; it is under no obligation to disclose reasons for a refusal (*The Times*, 6 Apr. 1978:6). But there is precious little by way of leverage or persuasion that the Board of Control has at its disposal in trying to influence Parliament or civil servants; the most it could hope for would be a polite hearing, without commitment. The same is true of a whole variety of professional 'talking shops': the Society of Education Officers, the Association of University Teachers, the British Association for the Advancement of Science, the Royal Town Planning Institute, the Shipbuilders' and Repairers' National Association, the Institution of Municipal Engineers, and many many others. Bodies such as these may well press their views very strongly, and may be aided by political support beyond Whitehall. In 1977 the Country Landowners' Association, a body of strong Conservative views which represents 40,000 landowners in England and Wales, and which is generally regarded as the least inhibited section of the farming lobby, congratulated Mr John Silkin, Labour's Minister of Agriculture, on learning that the government had decided to reject the Layfield Committee's recommendation that rates be levied upon farmland and farm buildings (*The Times*, 20 May 1977:4). This 'victory', however, was almost certainly not due to the representations of the Association (whose congratulations were an embarrassment to the government), but to the submissions of the National Farmers' Union and the government's minority position in the House of Commons.

There are, however, two types of sectional interest with special status and special powers. Firstly, there are a number of official or semi-official bodies with entrenched and well-defined rights of access and consultation. The most important of these are the nationalized-industry consumer 'watchdog' bodies (such as the Post Office Users' National Council, the regional Gas Consumers' Councils, and the area Electricity Consultative Councils), and the local government associations. Secondly, there are bodies representing special sectional interest, such as the Child Poverty Action Group.

The consumer watchdog bodies in the public sector are established by Act of Parliament. By law, the relevant nationalized industries must inform them of important changes in policy, such as charges and conditions of use, and give them time to comment on and make representations about such proposals. From time to time they are effective in bringing proposals to the notice of the media and of Parliament. But they are really toothless bulldogs, able to bark but not bite. In 1979 a report commissioned from the Public Interest Research Centre by the London Electricity Consultative Council and the Electricity Consumers' Council claimed that consumer consultative councils in the nationalized industries were ineffective because they lacked independent resources and adequate information; it claimed that the area electricity boards hoodwinked the public, supplying the consumer councils with too much irrelevant information and too little information that might be useful to them in monitoring the boards' activities (Medawar 1979).

The local government associations are in a very different situation. In 1974, following the reorganization of local government in England and Wales, the old-established Association of Municipal Corporations (dating from 1873) and the County Councils Association (1889) were replaced by the Association of Metropolitan Authorities and the Association of County Councils. At the same time a new District Councils Association was formed. London has its own London Boroughs Association. The links between these associations and the Department of the Environment are very strong. In April 1973, when the Water Bill was being considered by the Commons, a discussion arose in standing committee as to the future limits of responsibility of local authorities and regional water authorities for sewerage and sewage disposal. The Minister of Local Government, Graham Page, informed the committee that this matter had already been settled by 'model heads of agreement ... drawn up between my Department and the associations' (*Standing Committee D*, 3 Apr. 1973: cols. 693–768). Not even those members of the standing committee who had agreed to act as spokesmen for the local authority associations knew that such negotiations had taken place.

In comparing the nationalized industries' consumer councils and the local authority associations one moves, therefore, from general impotence to real power and privilege. In considering special sectional interests the same phenomenon is observed. There are some such groups which wield great authority or are widely recognized as being able to make representations on behalf of those whose interests they serve, or whose prestige and expertise is such that whatever they say will be listened to attentively. There are others whose rights to hear and to be heard, if recognized at all, are in practice constrained within narrow limits.

As examples of the former we may cite the National Society for the Prevention of Cruelty to Children, the British Legion and the British Limbless Ex-Servicemen's Association, the motoring organizations, and the National Federation of Old Age Pensioners' Associations. This group also includes some religious bodies, such as the Board of Deputies of British Jews and the British Union Conference of Seventh Day Adventists (both of which have statutory recognition and are regularly consulted on matters affecting adherents of the faiths they represent), and the major organizations representing ethnic minorities, such as the West Indian Standing Conference and the National Federation of Pakistani Associations. Groups such as these possess either prestige or respectability or both, and they provide unique services to society, on the basis of which they feel able to make claims upon it. The National Society for the Prevention of Cruelty to Children knows that its views will always be heard, and that it will invariably be consulted on matters affecting child abuse. It is *almost* an official body. Indeed in October 1981, in the face of huge deficits and a steep increase in instances of child battering, it announced its intention to seek at least £250,000 a year from the government as part of a substantial and regular grant. Dr Alan Gilmour, its Director, declared that in Kent, some London boroughs, and parts of the Midlands, the Society was the only agency of its kind providing a 24-hour service. 'If the society were to withdraw its service', he was reported as having declared, 'there would be no one to take its place' (*The Times*, 6 Oct. 1981:3). The sanction implied here could not be more obvious.

But other sectional interests are not half as powerful. Some are regarded as too radical or *avant-garde*, and the difficulties they experience in getting their views across, in public or in relation to central or local government, stem partly from this fact. Preservation of the Rights of Prisoners ('PROP') and Radical Alternatives to Prison ('RAP') are at the moment (1982) in this position. From time to time black-power groups make the headlines, such as the 'Black Eagles', who appeared on London's Portobello Road in the summer of 1970, and the Racial Adjustment Action Society, whose President, Malcolm X, became one of Britain's leading Black Muslims (*Sunday Telegraph*, 2 Aug. 1970:13). The Paedophile Information Exchange (founded 1974), whose object is to campaign for the legal and social acceptance of 'paedophile love', has failed not because it is not taken seriously (it is) but because it represents far too radical and outrageous a challenge to very widely held views in society. The Legalise Cannabis Campaign is scarcely less handicapped in its endeavours, and has claimed to have experienced considerable difficulty in placing advertisements in newspapers and magazines owned by the International Publishing Corporation (*The Times*, 21 Oct. 1978:2). There is little such groups can do to improve their bargaining position, except perhaps to take to the streets, as a number of black-power groups have done, in order to publicise their causes or to engage in physical-force methods.

We must now turn from sectional groups to cause groups. There is a tendency to define cause groups very widely, as a category into which all philanthropic groups can be conveniently placed. My definition is a deliberately narrow one. A cause group is a group whose object is to champion a cause, belief or dogma not associated with the vested interests of any particular section of the community. Thus I do not include in this category bodies such as the Child Poverty Action Group or the National Society for the Prevention of Cruelty to Children or, for that matter, groups such as Age Concern, Shelter, the Disablement Income Group, the motoring organizations, or the numerous ratepayers' and tenants' associations to be found throughout the land. These groups are clearly sectional interests, concerned to advance the interests of a particular section of the population; the use of the word 'sectional' here is technical only, and has no moral or ethical overtones. Cause groups advance general propositions for the sake of society as a whole.

Now there are obviously some groups which perform both functions. The Society of Teachers Opposed to Physical Punishment ('STOPP') is primarily concerned to campaign to outlaw corporal punishment in British schools; but it also investigates individual cases of what it regards as excessive physical punishment, and gives advice to teachers and parents. The Civic Trust lobbies government and Parliament in favour of the protection of the environment from the physical effects of heavy goods vehicles; this, however, leads it to campaign also for particular by-passes around sensitive towns, as well as for stricter controls generally upon noise, fumes and vibration. The Council for the Protection of Rural England plays a similar dual role. It promotes the sanctity of the countryside generally, but will also join in specific campaigns to protect particular environments (*The Times*, 15 Jan. 1982:2). The motoring organizations advance general causes, such as road safety, but also seek to protect the individual interests of their members. The Consumers' Association gives advice to its members on consumer problems, and sometimes agrees to fight cases through the courts. But it also campaigns for greater protection for the general body of consumers; in recent years one of its major successes has been the enactment of the Unfair Contract Terms Act (1977), under which some unfair conditions in contracts are automatically void even if the contract has been signed.

But, while accepting that hybrid groups such as these do exist to perform a dual role, it is evident that cause groups proper campaign only at the level of ideas and beliefs. They are not concerned, or are only very incidentally concerned, with the individual. An excellent example of a cause group is the British Maritime League, whose formation was mooted in January 1982 but whose existence and aims were put into dramatic perspective by the crisis caused by the Argentinian invasion of the Falkland Islands the following April. The object of the League is to 'fight naval cuts and campaign for greater public recognition of Britain's reliance on sea-power' (*The Times*, 21 May 1982:3). At its foundation it enjoyed the support of senior politicians of all major parties, of industrialists, retired admirals and a leading trade unionist, Mr Frank Chapple, general secretary of the Electrical, Electronic, Telecommunication and Plumbing Union.

But the principles a cause group espouses may not concern British society at all. Some of the most powerful cause groups fight on behalf of foreign interests. The British Zionist Federation and the Council for the Advancement of Arab–British Understanding spend very large sums of money each year not merely upon propaganda for the Jewish and Arab causes in the Middle East, but also in persuading parliamentarians and leaders of public opinion to adopt positions of sympathy and support for their respective views of this conflict. Each side has formal and informal links with MPs, and maintains contact with the media through meetings, letter-writing campaigns, advertisements and personal initiatives. While much of this work is carried on by official organizations, some of it is informal and unorganized: that is, there are plenty of Jewish and Arab sympathisers who take it upon themselves to make charges against the other side, and to deliver counter-charges, without waiting for or even bothering about official initiatives. The Israeli and Arab lobbies are, in fact, far wider than membership of the 'peak' organizations would suggest.

Indeed, the study of cause groups shows dramatically how dangerous it is to speak of pressure groups only in an organized sense. Propaganda by British Jews on behalf of Soviet Jewry, by Polish and Ukranian exiles on behalf of their compatriots in eastern Europe, or by Iranians in Britain on behalf of or in opposition to the rule of Ayattolah Khomeini, owe much to individual initiative which it would be wrong to suppose is always orchestrated. In the 1950s and 1960s there was a distinct 'pro-hanging' lobby opposed to the aims of those who sought to abolish capital punishment. 'Official groups such as the Home Office, party associations such as the National Union of Conservative Women, and certain fundamentalist religious organizations, although never welded together into a formal retentionist pressure group, nevertheless acted in a manner quite similar to one.' (Christoph, 1962:185)

However, the ability of a cause group to impose a sanction – and leaving out of the argument appeals to force, such as Iranians or Irish nationalists in Britain have sometimes resorted to – is almost invariably restricted. Cause groups do not produce goods which people want and cannot do without, or provide services which people need and must have. They cannot bring the nation to a halt. Their strength depends largely upon the amount of popular support they can muster.

Such support should not be underestimated. In a nation of animal-lovers, animal welfare groups such as the Royal Society for the Prevention of Cruelty to Animals and the League Against Cruel

Sports have no difficulty in finding a ready audience. Indeed, some animals are doubly fortunate, for they have pressure groups devoted exclusively to their interests. Sometimes, it is true, the aims of such groups are mixed. The British Horse Society speaks for the welfare of both horses and riders; it might be argued that the supporters of this Society are motivated to some extent by self-interest, or at least self-preservation (the Society wishes to make the wearing of safety helmets obligatory for horse and pony riders). But this cannot be said of the British Hedgehog Preservation Society, formed on the initiative of a retired major in Shropshire, in 1981, whose purpose appears to be to persuade local authorities to construct cattle grids in such a manner that hedgehogs may safely climb into and out of them (*The Times*, 23 Oct. 1982:1).

Yet campaigns on behalf of those who cannot campaign for themselves is certainly not confined to the animal kingdom. The Society for the Protection of Unborn Children can count on a minimum level of support in Catholic areas and has in several instances, such as at Ilford North in 1978 and at Crosby in 1981, succeeded in bringing the question of abortions into by-election campaigns. In 1966 a private citizen managed to poll a respectable 13.7 per cent of the votes by campaigning for the return of capital punishment for murder as a candidate in Nelson and Colne, the constituency of Mr Sydney Silverman, the architect of the legislation the previous year abolishing the death penalty for this offence. The Anti-Apartheid Movement has a strong and highly-motivated following which (especially in a sporting context) the media rarely ignore. The Electoral Reform Society (founded 1884) has succeeded for nearly a century in ensuring that the merits of proportional representation, and in particular of the single transferable vote system, have not been lost sight of; although proportional representation has not yet been adopted generally for United Kingdom parliamentary elections, it is used in Northern Ireland local elections and by many private organizations. In short, although cause groups depend far less on tangible sanctions and far more on winning converts, often through the skilful deployment of moral arguments, and although they are the most difficult pressure groups to organize and sustain, their impact can be very substantial.

Cause groups and sectional groups differ as to the ends they have in view and the means at their disposal to achieve those ends. But some of the most dramatic differences are to be found in the spheres of membership and organization. Because sectional groups are concerned to protect vested interests, they generally display a single-mindedness of purpose which makes for a strong degree of unity. In peak confederations, such as the Confederation of British Industry, this pattern can certainly break down. But elsewhere it is not only evident, but is often supported by a legislative framework. Pharmaceutical chemists must belong to and be registered with the Pharmaceutical Society of Great Britain, because of the compulsory provisions of the Pharmacy Act of 1954; the original voluntary nature of the Society (incorporated by royal charter in 1843) has quite disappeared since, under the provisions of the 1954 Act the Society now has the legal obligation placed upon it of maintaining a register of pharmaceutical chemists, and of conducting examinations, or granting exemptions, for the purpose of determining whether a chemist may be registered. The relationship between the General Medical Council (which registers medical practitioners and exercises a compulsory jurisdiction over them) and the British Medical Association (which elects representatives onto the General Medical Council) is such that membership of the Association is essential for any general practitioner who wishes to influence Council policy. A doctor does not have to belong to the Association; but there is a strong incentive for him to join.

This same phenomenon is observable in the trade unions. Leaving aside those unions, such as the railway unions, which have negotiated closed-shop agreements, even in the absence of such agreements there will often be compelling reasons for joining a trade union. Many unions have 'sole negotiating rights' with employers; they and they alone are recognized by employers for the purpose of agreeing rates of pay and conditions of service. To have any influence on such negotiations, employees must be prepared to join the appropriate unions and make their views known through them.

Membership of a sectional group can also bring material advantages. Allen Potter gives the example, dating from 1950, of members of pigs clubs registered with the Small Pig Keepers' Council, who received a larger amount of rationed feeding stuffs, for their pigs, compared with the amount allowed to pig-keepers who were not members of the Council (Potter 1961:95). Many trade unions negotiate special tax allowances with the Inland Revenue, and almost all professional bodies offer their members a range of services free or at much reduced rates. University teachers who belong to the Association of University Teachers receive automatic legal liability insurance and access to free legal advice. Members of the Consumers' Association have at their disposal, and for the payment of a small additional fee, the services of experienced personnel dealing with consumer problems; legal cases may be fought by the Association on their behalf. The motoring organizations offer a comparable range of services.

None of this means that a sectional group will necessarily achieve a complete or very high membership proportion, except where membership is enforced by statute or industrial practice. But it does mean that there will be strong forces within a sectional group making for central cohesion. This has implications for the way any sectional group operates. Because membership is more stable, and because there are incentives to obtain and retain membership, the income of such a group is more predictable and less prone to sharp and sudden fluctuations. In general, the only sectional groups which have to make public appeals for funds are those where the 'section' whose interests are protected is too poor to be able to fund the group itself: the disabled and infirm, the old and the young, the disadvantaged. Cause groups, by contrast, must *always* devote some of their energies to fund-raising; this itself diverts manpower and resources from other and perhaps more urgent tasks. And because the financial bases of most sectional groups are more secure, they will be able the more easily to afford permanent offices and paid full-time personnel.

Finally, we must note that many sectional groups possess the ability to impose sanctions internally as well as externally. The Trades Union Congress, and most trade unions, have the right of expulsion, as do a great many professional bodies, though there may be a right of appeal to some higher body, such as the Privy Council or the High Court. Since advantages accrue to individual members of these organizations derived solely from membership of them, the threat of expulsion carries a great deal of weight. But although some cause groups can impose sanctions on wayward members, these sanctions carry little more than moral force and can easily damage the organization which imposes them as much as the individual against whom they are directed. Disaffected members of cause groups can set up rival organizations whenever they choose. For members of sectional groups, secession if often totally impracticable.

From the foregoing comparison two general observations may be made about cause groups. The first is that, because they depend on voluntarism and not self-interest, cause groups often experience difficulties in finding the income to promote their causes. Some cause groups find wealthy backers to help them out. 'Aims' (formerly Aims of Industry), which exists to promote the virtues of private enterprise and to campaign against state ownership of industry, can expect hefty donations from private capital. But cause groups which have no vested interests behind them, such as the Lord's Day Observance Society, or the United Kingdom Alliance for the Total Suppression of the Liquor Traffic by the Will of the People, are forced to lead much more modest existences. Some may find a monied patron, and some may have the good fortune to receive legacies from well-wishers. In 1929 the Eugenics Society (founded, under a slightly different name, in 1907 'to foster a responsible attitude to parenthood') received a substantial legacy from one Henry Twitchin, who had become interested in the Society's work 'partly through his experiences as a large stock-breeder in Australia, and partly owing to the unsoundness of his own parentage' (Eugenics Society *Annual Report*, 1930–1, quoted in Potter 1961:152). The Society's income from investments enables it to offer membership, including use of its extensive specialist library, receipt of its quarterly bulletin, and attendance at its annual symposia and lectures, for the remarkably low fee (1981) of £2 per annum. It also supports research by appointing its own Research Fellow and by funding approved research projects.

Cause groups which are generally reckoned to be 'good causes', such as the Royal National Lifeboat Institution, can expect to attract substantial legacy income. Those groups which exist to promote friendly relations between the United Kingdom and a foreign country usually receive some form of assistance from the government of the foreign country concerned; the British government acts similarly towards anglophil societies abroad (Potter 1961:154). Some cause groups may receive grants from charitable trusts, such as the Ford and Nuffield Foundations. In 1977 the Anti-Nazi League was launched with the aid of a grant from the Rowntree Trust, which financed the League's only paid official, its organizing secretary (Alderman 1978). A few specially-favoured cause groups receive government grants. In 1961 Allen Potter listed the Royal Society for the Prevention of Accidents, the National Council of Social Service, the Central Council of Physical Recreation and the British Standards Institution among those pressure groups in receipt of public money; some cause groups are similarly supported by local authorities. But it is obvious that such support is dependent upon 'good behaviour'; and for that reason it is not an avenue open to most cause groups, particularly if the causes they espouse are not popular.

This leads to a consideration of the second general difference between cause and sectional groups, namely the types of membership which each attracts. Most sectional groups are in the fortunate position of having 'captive' memberships; even where membership of an appropriate sectional group is not legally obligatory, there will generally be very strong economic or professional pressures to join, and there will be membership fees to be paid. Partly as a consequence, sectional groups tend to have democratic structures and constitutions, even if (as is the case with many trade unions) the active membership tends to be alarmingly small; the opportunity to participate in decision-making exists, though it is often not exercised.

But a great many cause groups remain 'self-appointed committees' (Potter 1961:127). They have supporters, subscribers or benefactors rather than participating members. The Campaign for Nuclear Disarmament in the 1950s deliberately dispensed with 'members', for it was felt that membership would provide too many opportunities for infiltration by other organizations (Potter 1961:128). The Anti-Nazi League has a self-appointed steering committee (a majority of which are Labour MPs) but no members; one can become a 'supporter' of the League, on payment of £1, but not a member. Mike Daube, of Action on Smoking and Health ('ASH'), asserts that the most effective pressure groups tend to be those which are managed by 'a small highly professional core: members can be useful (not least in paying subscriptions) but they can also be a hindrance and often fail to realize that time spent servicing them could have been spent more profitably' (Daube 1979). This does not, of course, mean that cause groups lack mass appeal. Both the Campaign for Nuclear Disarmament and the Anti-Nazi League have attracted very large followings. It does mean that the day-to-day work of such groups rests with small numbers of individuals who are not, as it happens, publicly accountable; their policy decisions do not have to be endorsed by wider 'constituencies', though, obviously, should they strike out on a particularly narrow road they will find their supporters melting away.

Many cause groups are, therefore, oligarchies and nothing else: the oligarchy *is* the group. Membership rolls, where they exist, tend to be small. The membership of the Abortion Law Reform Association never reached more than about 2,000. At its height, in 1955–56, the National Campaign for the Abolition of Capital Punishment boasted around 30,000 *supporters*, but this was quite exceptional, and short-lived; in later years regular paying supporters of the National Campaign amounted to only a few hundred (Pym 1974:61–2). Those who lead cause groups are generally much freer than those who lead sectional groups to do more or less as they please. At the same time, since cause groups depend heavily on public sympathy for their effectiveness, the quality of the leadership is of paramount importance. The National Campaign had Victor Gollancz as Chairman and Gerald Gardiner, Q.C., and Arthur Koestler on its executive. Action Aid, an organization which seeks to persuade those with charitable inclinations to sponsor individual children in poor countries, has secured the former Conservative minister and athlete Christopher Chataway as its Honorary Treasurer, and uses his photograph and signature in its literature. The Anti-Nazi League benefited from having the actress and television personality Miriam Karlin on its steering committee. The famous comedy actor Brian Rix is Secretary General of 'MENCAP', the National Society for Mentally Handicapped Children and Adults.

Cause groups, then, have to work harder for their income and are much more sensitive to popular whims. 'Success' or 'failure' is often irrelevant to the fortunes of a sectional group; a particular campaign may be won or lost, but self-interest will ensure the group's survival. But for a cause group the loss of one battle can be crucial. All in all, cause groups lead precarious lives. The byeways of British politics are littered with causes that have failed.

Chapter three
PRESSURE GROUPS AND POLITICIANS

All pressure groups make political demands, because politics is concerned with the allocation of resources and the ordering of society. Every pressure group must therefore expect to have to operate in the political arena as well as in the administrative machinery of central or local government. Many will also have to operate in a public arena. Purely local pressure groups will probably be content to confine their political activities to the town-hall. But national groups will wish to make their presence felt in and around the Palace of Westminster; it is with these activities that this chapter is mainly concerned.

However 'neutral' a pressure group may appear to be, or may wish to be, few groups can afford the luxury of being 'above politics'. Most like to think of themselves as unaligned – at least in theory – because this gives them greater flexibility and is a form of insurance against changes of government. There is also a belief that unaligned groups are accorded greater respect, particularly by the media and civil servants, and that this respect might well be a factor determining the eventual success or failure of a particular campaign. Mike Daube has argued that a pressure-group campaign must be non-partisan: 'a politically committed campaigner may win a few short-term battles, but is unlikely to be trusted by civil servants, journalists, or politicians of other parties, and can be fairly easily discredited' (Daube 1979). But he adds that 'people who stand in the middle of the road must expect to be run over'. There is no doubt that a partisan group enjoys advantages, at least of access, when its party is in power; political virginity is sacrificed, but cohabitation is expected to bring its own unique rewards. In recent years, indeed, there appears to have been a greater readiness on the part of previously non-aligned groups to compromise their neutrality in party matters. The picturesque world of the fox-hunt is now a political minefield, with the Hunt Saboteurs' Association and the League

Against Cruel Sports identified with the politics of the radical left and the British Field Sports Society and the British Equestrian Federation identified with the Conservative Party, which is opposed to the legal prohibition of field sports (*The Times*, 24 May 1982:3; 31 May:4).

Do pressure groups with a political affiliation receive especially favourable treatment, and is the sacrifice of political neutrality worthwhile? In trying to answer these questions the relationship between the trade unions and the Labour Party looms large in the discussion. For here is a case of pressure groups actually creating a political party to serve their own ends. The Labour Representation Committee was established in 1900 following a decision of the Trades Union Congress the previous year. The trade unions were fearful of the consequences of judge-made law in the 1890s, because a series of judicial decisions had eroded their powers of strike action and peaceful picketing; they hoped that the entry into Parliament, under the auspices of the Labour Representation Committee, of a significant number of working-class MPs would bring pressure to bear upon the government to grant them sweeping immunities from criminal prosecution.

In 1906, with the passage of the Trade Disputes Act by the new Liberal government, this hope was realized. Throughout this century the trade union movement has used the Labour Party to bolster its privileges. In 1913 the right of the unions to institute a voluntary political levy upon their members (a right denied in the Osborne judgment of 1909) was guaranteed by law. In 1967 the iron and steel industry, denationalized by the Conservatives in 1953, was taken once more under state control, as the Trades Union Congress wished, by a Labour government. A few years later another Labour administration repealed much of the Conservative Industrial Relations Act of 1971 and replaced it with new legislation, the Trade Unions and Labour Relations Act (1974) and the Employment Protection Act (1975), thus giving the trade unions more powers than they had ever enjoyed hitherto.

These few examples certainly support the argument that the British trade union movement has done well from its special relationship with the Labour Party. Those who argue that this relationship is too close ignore history and fail to understand how the Labour Party came into being; either the party is the political arm of the trade union movement, or it is nothing. Three-quarters of the central income of the party is derived from trade-union affiliation fees, and this financial support is reflected in the so-called 'card vote' at

Labour conferences, whereby each union has a voting strength based upon its affiliated membership; he who pays the piper calls the tune. At present there are fifty affiliated unions, representing over 6 million workers; the two largest, the Transport and General Workers' Union and the Amalgamated Union of Engineering Workers, have over a million members each. Thus, out of a total party membership of about 7 millions (in 1980) the affiliated unions necessarily dominate all party conference proceedings. Moreover, in the electoral college arrangement agreed upon in 1981 for choosing the Leader of the party, 40 per cent of the votes are directly controlled by the trade unions, to say nothing of union influence within local constituency parties.

Not content with exercising the major influence in shaping the destinies of the party they created, trade unions also sponsor individual MPs. Such sponsorship has a long history. In the late nineteenth century the miners regularly put up parliamentary candidates, usually under the Liberal banner; the first two working-class MPs, Alexander McDonald and Thomas Burt (both returned to Parliament in 1874), were elected in this way. The National Union of Teachers began to sponsor and assist parliamentary candidates in 1895, and in 1909 the National Farmers' Union established a Parliamentary Fund, with the object of securing the return to the House of Commons of 'a few practical working farmers' (Stewart 1957: 173). From time to time other unions and trade or professional associations have also sought to sponsor candidates for Parliament. From 1918 to 1945 the Educational Institute of Scotland sponsored an MP and virtually controlled one of the Scottish university seats (Stewart 1957: 174).

But there is a world of difference between this kind of sponsorship and that engaged in by trade unions affiliated to the Labour Party. The National Farmers' Union, which ceased sponsoring candidates in 1945, disavowed any intention of seeking a party political attachment. Although all its sponsored MPs were Conservatives, it was their agricultural politics rather than their party politics which mattered most to members of the union. The National Union of Teachers has always aimed at achieving a balance in its parliamentary representation. Its sponsored and supported MPs have never totalled more than six. Before 1974 the teachers' union sponsored certain parliamentary candidates, who received a grant towards their election expenses; those elected were entitled to receive an allowance. The passage of the 1974 Trade Unions Act led to the cessation of this scheme, which could only have been continued by the establishment of a separate political fund. Now the union has a scheme which allows it to engage up to five MPs as 'Parliamentary Consultants'. In June 1975 four Labour MPs and one Conservative accepted invitations to act in this capacity. Union rules stipulate that all parliamentary consultants must, prior to their appointment, have been in membership of the National Union of Teachers for a period of not less than five years, or the whole of their teaching career. In choosing parliamentary consultants, regard must be paid 'to enlisting assistance both on the Government and Opposition sides of the House of Commons and to representation of constituents in both England and Wales'. Parliamentary consultants so appointed are expected to assist the union in parliamentary matters, but only 'within the bounds of Parliamentary practice and constitutional usage'; each parliamentary consultant receives an annual fee of £300.

Trade-union-sponsored MPs in the Labour Party are in a very different position. Because the party was founded by trade unions, its rules make specific provision for such sponsorship. A sponsoring union (which must, of course, be affiliated to the party) may contribute up to £350 towards the running costs of a borough constituency party, or £420 in a county constituency, plus 80 per cent of the candidate's election expenses and 65 per cent of the salary of an agent. At the general election of May 1979, out of 269 Labour candidates elected to Parliament, no less than 133 had been sponsored by trade unions; only 22 union-sponsored candidates had not been elected. In the new House of Commons 21 MPs had been sponsored by the Amalgamated Union of Engineering Workers, 20 by the Transport and General Workers, 16 by the National Union of Mineworkers, 14 by the General and Municipal Workers and 12 by the National Union of Railwaymen (Butler and Kavanagh 1979:288). These unions, indeed, enjoyed greater parliamentary representation than the Liberal Party, and can justly claim to be political entities in their own right.

Do union-sponsored MPs give value for money? And to what extent are the strings of the Parliamentary Labour Party pulled by the unions which, since 1945, have sponsored over 40 per cent of all successful Labour candidates? In trying to provide answers to these questions we might note at the outset that many of the sponsored candidates are not working class and may have only the slenderest connections with the trade or industry represented by their sponsoring unions. The best union brains tend to be directed towards full-time union administration; in 1979 only about a third of Labour MPs came from the working classes. Unions have tended to look to middle-class, university-trained professional men and women for sponsorship; in October 1974 60 of the 159 sponsored candidates possessed university qualifications. In recent years unions have also taken to sponsoring successful Labour MPs who do not have any previous experience of the unions sponsoring them. The Transport and General Workers has sponsored Peter Shore (Cambridge) and Dr Jeremy Bray (Cambridge and Harvard); in 1979 the National Union of Railwaymen sponsored Tam Dalyell (Cambridge; a teacher and political journalist) and Philip Whitehead (Oxford; a television producer).

Furthermore, although a union-sponsored MP will naturally be expected to put the union's point of view, both in the Commons and in the party, there is a point beyond which the sponsoring union has no control over his actions. The rules of parliamentary privilege protect a Member of Parliament from threats and crude manipulation by an outside body; at Westminster a Member is free to say what he thinks and to vote as he pleases. The definitive statement of this protection arose, in the 1940s, out of the political activities of two unions, the National Union of Distributive and Allied Workers and the Civil Service Clerical Association. In 1944 the National Union, at the request of the St Helens Labour Party, asked its 'Political General Secretary', the St Helens Labour MP W. A. Robinson, to resign from Parliament; when he refused, the Union withdrew from him its sponsorship and financial support. The matter was referred to the House of Commons' Committee on Privileges, which declared that 'the payment to, or receipt by, a Member [of Parliament] of money or the offer or acceptance of other advantage, for promoting or opposing a particular proceeding or measure, constitutes an undoubted breach of privilege' (House of Commons Papers of 1943–4, No.85:5).

On that occasion the Commons declined to take the matter further. But three years later the Privileges Committee deliberated on the celebrated case of W. J. Brown, Independent MP for Rugby. Since 1923 W. J. Brown had been General Secretary of the Civil Service Clerical Association. In 1942, on his election to Parliament, his union gave him the title of Political General Secretary, confirmed that he would continue to receive a salary, and entered into an agreement with him specifying his duties, obliging him to deal with all questions concerning the Association which might require parliamentary or political action, but confirming also his complete freedom to engage in political activities (House of Commons Papers of 1946–7, No.118:59–60). In the course of time Brown and his union fell out, and the union's Executive Committee decided to terminate the agreement with him. He appealed to the protection of Parliament. The Privileges Committee inquired into the matter, and subsequently the House of Commons approved a motion to the following effect (HC Debates 15. July 1947:col.365):

> That this House agrees with the Report of the Committee on Privileges, and in particular declares that it is inconsistent with the dignity of the House, with the duty of a member to his constituents, and with the maintenance of the privilege of freedom of speech, for any Member of the House to enter into any contractual agreement with an outside body, controlling or limiting the Member's complete independence and freedom of action in Parliament or stipulating that he shall act in any way as the representative of such outside body in regard to any matters to be transacted in Parliament; the duty of a Member being to his constituents and to the country as a whole, rather than to any particular section thereof.

The most that a union which is dissatisfied with its sponsored MP can do is to intimate that he might not be reselected for sponsorship at the next general election. Even this course of action has its dangers. In June 1975 the Yorkshire Area Council of the National Union of Mineworkers resolved that 'No Miners' MP shall actively campaign or work against the Union policy' on major issues. What these issues might be was not specified, but it was well known that the Yorkshire Area Council was displeased at the support for British entry into the Common Market given by one of its sponsored MPs, the Labour minister Roy Mason, whom it threatened with withdrawal of sponsorship. The matter was smoothed over when the Committee on Privileges received an assurance from the President of the miners' union to the effect that the union did not accept the views of the Yorkshire Area on the supposed obligations of sponsorship (*The Times*, 26, 28 June 1975:1). But two years later the issue surfaced again, this time in a much more acute form. In May 1977 the annual conference of the National Union of Public Employees resolved to instruct its six sponsored MPs to refuse to support Labour government cuts in public expenditure; there was a strong hint that sponsorship would be withdrawn if this instruction was not obeyed. By an overwhelming majority the Commons decided to refer this matter to its Privileges Committee, which rebuked the union in unequivocal and definitive language (*The Times*, 29 July 1977:4):

> To withdraw [the Committee wrote to the union], or threaten to withdraw, a member's sponsorship in the circumstances set out in the

> [conference] resolution would constitute a serious contempt of the House.
>
> * * * *
>
> In any conflict between the loyalty owed by a member to Parliament and that he might owe to some other person or organization, the law of Parliament requires the member's loyalty to Parliament to prevail. There is an obligation upon any person or organization who enters into a contractual relationship with an MP, just as there is upon the member, to make themselves aware of the law of Parliament as it affects such relationships.

But, quite apart from the constitutional constraints to sponsorship, there is surprisingly little evidence that the sponsorship of MPs has bestowed upon sponsoring unions advantages or benefits which they might not have obtained by other means. The 1906 Trade Disputes Act was passed by a Liberal government in no way dependent on the support of the thirty Labour MPs then in the House of Commons. The great social and industrial reforms of 1945–51 were carried through by a Labour parliamentary party in which union-sponsored MPs accounted for less than a third of the Party's total.

Since then, there has been only one major instance in which it could be argued that sponsorship has brought tangible rewards. In 1969, following the report of the Donovan Commission which it had established four years previously, the Labour government published a White Paper, *In Place Of Strife*, in which sweeping reform of industrial relations law was proposed, including compulsory ballots before unions might call strikes and compulsory 'cooling off' periods before strike action might be invoked, with penal sanctions against recalcitrant unions. The trade-union movement mounted a ferocious campaign against these proposals, and set about lobbying Labour MPs. In a vote in the Commons on 3 March 1969, 103 Labour MPs abstained or voted against *In Place of Strife*. Abortive negotiations between the government and the Trades Union Congress then followed. In June the Labour Chief Whip, Bob Mellish, was called to Downing Street to tell the Cabinet that a Bill, based upon the White Paper, would not pass that session. The proposals were dropped.

It is tempting to see in these events a justification for sponsorship. Such a judgment would be entirely unwarranted. It is true that sponsored MPs were to be found in the forefront of the battle against the White Paper; of the fifty-three Labour MPs who had voted against the White Paper, twenty-six were union-sponsored (Muller

1977:84). But Mr Wilson's government was in deep political trouble anyway, and had already enraged the trade unions, and its own left wing, by its statutory wages policy; the Prime Minister's leadership of his party was itself under attack. What sealed the Bill's fate was the attitude of Labour's National Executive Committee, which on 26 March 1969 came out against industrial relations legislation based upon the White Paper; this was a clear indication that the party and the government were at loggerheads. As a result, many Labour MPs opposed legislation less because they objected to the White Paper than as a result of their wish to preserve party unity.

In a wider sense, there can be no question but that the trade unions have reaped advantages from affiliation to the Labour Party. Many of Labour's policies originate in motions put forward by trade-union delegates to the party's annual conferences; some of these policies eventually find their way onto the statute book. The passage of the Equal Pay Acts of 1970 and 1975 was due in large measure to the persistent lobbying of Labour administrations by the General Council of the Trades Union Congress. The trade-union movement can also claim to have provided the impetus for the 1975 Sex Discrimination Act, which made it unlawful to discrimination on grounds of sex in the fields of employment, education, housing, goods and services, and which created an Equal Opportunities Commission to investigate discrimination in these fields.

Nor can there be any doubt that sponsorship of MPs brings influence with it. When details of important Bills are being discussed, such as nationalization or pensions, it is very useful to have at Westminster an advocate who will make it his business to bring a particular union's viewpoint to the attention of the Commons. But though sponsorship may bring access and influence, it does not bestow power upon the sponsor. Professor Muller, in his exhaustive study of union-sponsored MPs, concludes that the attempt of the Labour Party's Trade Union Group 'to act as the corporate agent of the unions in Parliament has not been very effective . . . As a private organization of union-sponsored MPs, it became increasingly a social club, held together by nostalgia for a shared common experience in the factory or mine' (Muller 1977:87).

As we shall see, there are many organizations which do not sponsor MPs but which have no difficulty in making their views known in Parliament, and at far less cost. To use a sponsored MP in an overtly partisan manner may also detract from the merit of what is being put forward. Sometimes it is better than a Member without trade-union links should be allowed to put forward what is in effect a trade-union case. And the money used for sponsorship could easily be paid directly to the Labour Party, which the unions dominate anyway because of the block vote. Why, then, do trade unions continue to sponsor parliamentary candidates? The answer seems to lie in tradition and status. Unions feel that the sponsorship system is one means of ensuring some genuine working-class representation in the Commons. A sponsored MP is a symbol of political authority, and an assurance to union members that the political levy they pay is buying something worthwhile.

Other political parties do not allow sponsorship of MPs. It is not possible for organizations such as trade unions to become affiliated to the Conservative Party, and Conservative candidates and MPs are not permitted to make more than nominal annual donations to their local parties; constituency Conservative associations must meet all their election expenses out of subscriptions and fund-raising activities. The Social Democratic Party only permits individual membership, and stresses that SDP MPs cannot be 'mandated' or subject to direction or control by any organ of the party. Although the constitution of the Social Democratic Party permits the recognition of 'Associated Organizations', which could in theory include trade unions or professional bodies, the membership of any such organization must be limited to members of the party or sympathetic non-members; and a recognized associated organization has no right of representation in the party's Consultative Assembly.

But it is perfectly possible for pressure groups to buy their way into political parties which do not permit sponsorship. The Conservative Party relies very heavily upon donations from the worlds of business and commerce. On average, Conservative Party headquarters can expect to raise about £1 million annually from business gifts; this represents approximately two-thirds of the party's annual income (Alderman 1978a:53). Since the reform of company law in 1967, it has been possible to identify the precise source of many of these donations. According to researches undertaken by the Labour Party, some of the biggest donations have come from the building firm Taylor Woodrow, the Rank Organization and Trafalgar House, owners of the *Daily Express, Sunday Express* and *Daily Star* (*Daily Telegraph*, 8 Sept. 1979:8). Other donations are not made directly to the Conservative Party, but to 'independent' pressure groups whose aims broadly coincide with Conservative philosophy: British United Industrialists, which *The Times* has described as 'a group of businessmen committed to free enterprise through publicity, research and financing other groups with the same aims'; the Economic League; the National Association for Freedom; and Aims (see *The Times*, 26 Aug. 1978:2; and Ch. 5, below). Of course, business donations to the Conservative Party no more guarantee political compliance than do trade-union donations to Labour. Differences between the Trades Union Congress and Labour governments in the late 1960s and mid–1970s over wage restraint have been mirrored by sharp disagreements between the Confederation of British Industry and the Conservative administration elected in May 1979 over general economic strategy. But such donations do give big business a foot in the door of Conservative Central Office. The Conservative Party, for its part, could not do without them. And their value has been recognized by the Social Democratic Party which, early in its life, began persuading the business community 'to back the infant party with hard cash as well as votes' (*Sunday Times*, 6 Sept. 1981:60).

There is, however, a much easier, and cheaper, way by which pressure groups can enter the political process. To sponsor a parliamentary candidate, or to make a hefty donation to a party, involves a political as well as a financial risk: for if one's candidate or one's party is unsuccessful, credibility as well as money may be lost. It is far better to wait until after an election has been held, and then to approach sympathetic MPs with offers of what are termed 'consultancies'; these range from agreements to liaise informally to signed contracts involving the payment of fees or honoraria.

Sometimes a group is fortunate in that one or more of its members may be elected to the Commons, or obtain a peerage. The legal professions are always well represented at Westminster; the Parliament elected in 1979 contained 95 barristers and solicitors, 70 of them in the Conservative Party. But the number of parliamentary lawyers has often been much higher. In 1967 the Institute of Directors boasted that over 250 members of both Houses of Parliament were also members of the Institute. 'They can be counted on to see that the views of directors are adequately voiced in Parliament and their interests protected whenever the occasion demands it' (quoted in Madgwick 1976:276). In 1982, 22 MPs and over 80 peers were Institute members; in addition a Conservative MP, Michael Grylls, acted as unpaid parliamentary spokesman. During the 1970s the total number of company directors and executives in the House of Commons averaged 85 and never fell below 70.

There will usually be 12 or so university teachers in Parliament, and occasionally as many as 24, of whom the majority (15 out of 21 in 1979) are likely to be on the Labour side; many of these retain their membership of the Association of University Teachers and can be relied upon to speak on its behalf. When the Association, in common with other campus unions, held a mass lobby of Parliament in November 1981, MPs who supported its protest against Conservative government policy towards the university sector included Robert Rhodes James, the Conservative MP for Cambridge and a distinguished academic historian. Just occasionally a salaried employee or former employee of an organization will become an MP. In 1950 the Secretary of the British Medical Association, Dr Charles Hill, was elected MP for Luton, though he resigned his post upon entering Parliament (Stewart 1957:153). In 1979 the Director of the Child Poverty Action Group, Frank Field, became Labour MP for Birkenhead; although he, too, resigned his post upon election, he has continued to campaign vigorously on behalf of the poor, and played a significant part in the debate on the 1980 Social Security Bill (Donnison 1981:174–5).

More commonly, however, organizations will wait until after an election and then approach MPs with offers of honorary or even of salaried positions. The Building Societies' Association has (1982) vice-presidents from the major political parties, including 5 MPs and 11 peers in addition to its President, Lord Selkirk. The major commercial associations, such as the National Chamber of Trade, appoint both MPs and peers from the major parties as honorary vice-presidents; in 1982 the National Chamber had 23 honorary vice-presidents in the House of Commons and 15 in the House of Lords. The British Legion actually has a branch in the House of Commons (Wootton 1957–44). In 1979 the Board of Deputies of British Jews elected as its President the Labour MP Greville Janner; his predecessors in this office have included his father, the Labour MP Barnet (later Lord) Janner (President 1955–64); the Conservative MP Michael Fidler (President 1967–73 and a Member of Parliament 1970–74); and the Labour peer Lord Fisher of Camden (President 1973–79).

We might note that, from the point of view of parliamentary advocacy, peers are often as acceptable to pressure groups as members of the House of Commons; indeed, since the formal parliamentary duties of peers are likely to be far less onerous, and their constituency duties non-existent, they are likely to take a more active interest in the affairs of organizations to which they are appointed. In addition a smattering of peers may also have certain advantages of prestige. The Automobile Association (1981) boasts two peers among its four vice-presidents and another peer (and former Conservative MP and Minister), Lord Erroll of Hale, as its Chairman.

The Labour peer and former MP Lord Houghton of Sowerby is well known for his support of animal welfare causes. In 1978 he was Vice-Chairman of the Royal Society for the Prevention of Cruelty to Animals and Chairman of the General Election Co-ordinating Committee for Animal Protection, a body which campaigned 'for the purpose of putting animals into politics' and, specifically, for legislation on a number of issues, including experiments on live animals and the export of live farm animals (*The Times*, 24 Oct. 1978:6). Three years later Lord Houghton introduced into the Lords a Slaughter of Animals Bill, with the object of prohibiting the export of carcasses of animals slaughtered by methods which did not involve prior stunning. Though this Bill had no chance of becoming law, it provided publicity for the organizations behind it, and an opportunity for parliamentary dialogue on the issues involved. Since parliamentary Bills are printed at the public expense, the promotion of a Bill in this way, with the support of a conglomerate of pressure groups, must be reckoned exceedingly good value for money.

Sometimes, however, the relationship between a Member of Parliament and a pressure group will be more than merely honorary. Many groups find it expedient to appoint MPs as paid advisers or consultants. Contracts will be drawn up, carefully worded so as to avoid the prohibitions laid down by the Privileges Committee. There is of course a world of difference between an adviser or consultant and a spokesman or representative. But however carefully worded an agreement between a Member of Parliament and a pressure group may be, such an agreement is bound to give rise to the suspicion that money is disbursed for services of an advocatory nature: that the MP is 'in the pay' of the group he 'advises'.

In May 1972 the Labour MP Brian Walden entered into a five-year contract with the National Association of Bookmakers (NAB), for whom he agreed to act as a paid parliamentary consultant. Mr Walden apparently interpreted his role merely as that of an adviser on the workings of Parliament. But the NAB was at that time locked in battle with the Home Office, which had promoted a Bill to allow, *inter alia*, the state-owned Totalisator Board to open betting shops in competition with private betting shops. In what the *Daily Mail* described as 'one of the most blatant acts of lobbying', the NAB's Parliamentary Action Committee had lost no time in wining and dining large numbers of MPs from both sides of the House of Commons. The Conservative MP Sir Gerald Nabarro was reported to have torn up his invitation, calling it 'naked bribery'; but, as so often, Sir Gerald was in a decided minority. The Bill ran into serious trouble;

Mr Walden, in particular, opposed it root and branch. He had done so in February, when he had certainly had no financial interest in the bookmaking industry, and he continued to do so after entering into the contract which the NAB had offered him the following May. The bookmakers used the extraordinary length of the committee sittings on the Bill to wring concessions from the government, and Mr Walden appears to have acted as 'go-between' in the negotiations between the NAB and the Home Office. In due course the offending clause was drastically modified, so that there could be no doubt that the Totalisator Board was not going to be allowed to set up in direct competition with private bookmakers on anything like favourable terms. In effect the Bill was dead (Hoggart and Wallace 1974).

In this case it would be quite wrong to suppose that the relationship between Mr Walden and the NAB was in any way sinister. Mr Walden admitted his financial interest and, in any case, his own personal opposition to the Bill was but a factor of small importance in its eventual fate. A large number of Conservative MPs also disagreed with the proposal to allow the Totalisator Board to compete with 'off course' betting shops; even the Chairman of the Horse Race Levy Board, Lord Wigg, had his doubts. Mr Walden doubtless gave valuable and very proper advice on parliamentary tactics; but he was no 'secret weapon'.

However, a second example gives cause for genuine anxiety. In 1981 the tobacco industry faced a two-pronged attack from the anti-smoking lobby. A private member's Bill sought tighter legal control of the advertising of cigarettes. Whether such a bill would ever have reached the statute book is open to grave doubt. But the Under-Secretary of State at the Department of Health and Social Security, Sir George Younger, was known to be in favour of the statutory prohibition of tobacco and cigarette advertisements, and his boss the Secretary of State, Mr Patrick Jenkin, was known to be sympathetic to this idea. In 1980 Mr Jenkin had negotiated a voluntary agreement controlling cigarette advertising; the agreement was due to expire on 31 July 1982 and Mr Jenkin had made it clear that Parliament would then be free to review the voluntary agreement and, perhaps, to replace it with something less voluntary. If the private Member's Bill had been allowed to proceed, its successful passage through the Commons might have been used as evidence of parliamentary feeling on this subject. The tobacco industry therefore had to kill off the Bill and engineer the removal of the Minister and his Under-Secretary.

Both objectives were achieved. It happened that the tobacco Bill was preceded by one dealing with zoos. No less than 164 amendments to the zoos Bill were tabled, 87 of them by (among others) Sir Anthony Kershaw, Conservative MP for Stroud, a self-confessed adviser to British American Tobacco who has, quite properly, declared this connection in the voluntary register of MPs' interests. 'I am very interested in animals', Sir Anthony later declared on BBC Radio; but he added candidly that 'one of my interests in that particular Bill [the zoos Bill] was to keep out the Bill banning advertising on smoking which came afterwards'. The length of time taken to deal with the zoos Bill (five hours) ensured that the tobacco Bill was never reached.

Then, in the autumn, Sir George Younger and Mr Jenkin were removed from their posts. Dr Mike Daube, a former Director of ASH, and Adam Raphael, political editor of *The Observer*, both regarded this as a Downing Street response to pressure from the tobacco industry. Sir George had hoped to promote a government Bill to so extend the Medicines Act that cigarette and tobacco advertising might be controlled in the same way as advertisements for medicines. Following his departure from the Department of Health, this idea was abandoned. The new Minister of State, Dr Gerard Vaughan, declared at once that he had no plans for legislation and that a new voluntary agreement would be negotiated with the tobacco industry instead (Hetherington 1981:671; Daube 1981).

The double victory of the tobacco industry owed more to it than the retention of MPs' services. The tobacco lobby is a rich and powerful one. Tobacco duty represents an income to the Exchequer which in the financial year 1979–80 amounted to some £2,579.5 millions. The industry wisely channels large sums of money into sponsorship of sports, such as cricket and tennis, and it is possible that the withdrawal of such sponsorship might have been hinted at during the 1981 campaign; certainly, this was an allegation put to the Prime Minister in the House of Commons and which she never denied. But the fact remains that, according to Dr Daube's researches, thirty-two MPs have financial links either directly with the tobacco industry or with advertising and public relations firms which handle tobacco company accounts. (Freeman 1981). These MPs must be regarded as political arms of the industry, on whose wellbeing their own livelihoods in part depend.

Not all relationships between MPs and client groups are as mercenary as this. Many pressure groups are more than happy if they are able to form special relationships with just a handful of MPs, who will speak up for their interests, represent their views to the government, and perhaps ask the occasional parliamentary question on their behalf. In return, a Member who acts in this capacity can usually be assured of a constant source of reliable information on a particular area of government policy. For the ambitious parliamentarian, services of this sort may well lead to publicity and public recognition, especially if the pressure group on whose behalf he acts is well known or likely to be accorded substantial media coverage.

What manner of MPs may expect to be approached? Obviously, an identity of interest with the client pressure group is an advantage. Most MPs do not attempt to become specialists in every branch of government. Each has his particular interest, and close contact with the organizations catering for those interests will therefore be of mutual benefit. Such contacts encompass both domestic organizations and foreign governments. Many of these bodies are only marginally 'party political', if at all. The Consumers' Association provides briefs for debates on consumer affairs, the animal welfare organizations on animal topics. The Church of England's Council on Betting and Gaming makes its views on gambling known to interested MPs. In his survey of *British Members of Parliament* Professor A. King quotes a Member of Parliament describing his relationship with a group concerned with the passage of the Race Relations Bill in 1968 (King 1974:76–7):

> In 1968, on the committee stage of the Race Relations Bill, there was a body set up called Equal Rights, which did a very good briefing job of Members on the committee, and they were extremely well organised. Their views about the shape the legislation should take happened to accord with mine to a very large extent, and every morning at 9.30 when the committee was about to sit, one was briefed on what was coming up that day: both orally and with pieces of paper and so on. If they happened to be pushing a particular point that I disagreed with, I opted out. When I agreed with them, I did what I could. It was a total service: I went into that committee briefed on every amendment that was going to come up in a way that I've only ever seen a minister briefed or an opposition spokesman.

In this case the initiative came from a pressure group, which rightly concentrated its efforts on the committee stage of the Bill, where there usually lies the best chance of constructive amendment. This is invariably true of a government Bill. The government of the day is most unlikely to be defeated at the second-reading stage, when only the principle of the proposed legislation is under debate. But it may yield to criticism of details when, in committee, each clause is separately considered, often in a remarkably non-partisan manner.

Sometimes, however, a pressure group will be approached by a Member of Parliament. In December 1953 the National Smoke Abatement Society (founded 1929), which had been campaigning for tougher legal controls on atmospheric pollution, was approached by Gerald Nabarro, who had won first place in the ballot for private members' Bills that session. Mr Nabarro wished to introduce a Bill on smoke abatement, but needed the expertise of the Society in drafting the measure, and its financial assistance in meeting the expenses involved. He came to an agreement with the Society, and a Bill was introduced. Though it did not pass it attracted a great deal of parliamentary support and forced the government to act quickly, whereas in other circumstances ministers might have been expected (given the opposition of industrial interests) to play for time. The government introduced a Bill of its own, which became law as the Clean Air Act, 1956. During its passage, and particularly at the committee stage, Mr Nabarro acted as the Society's principal representative, though some of the Society's amendments were moved by the Labour MPs A. Blenkinsop and R. E. Winterbottom (Ashby and Anderson 1981:104–19).

An arrangement of a rather different kind is illustrated by reference to the policy of the Police Federation. In 1955 the Federation began to collect subscriptions from members, and decided to use this money to equip itself with expert assistance in the negotiations on pay and conditions of service which took place at the Police Council. An approach was made to the Labour MP for Cardiff South East, James Callaghan, who had been a junior minister under Clement Attlee and had, prior to that, worked with the Inland Revenue Staff Federation. In September 1955 Mr Callaghan was appointed the Police Federation's first Parliamentary Consultant. It was clear at the outset that his job entailed much more than negotiating on the Police Council. In 1956 he led a successful parliamentary campaign to induce the government to legislate for the back-dating of police pay awards. Following the 1959 general election he was offered a contract by the Federation, thus putting his relations with it on a more permanent footing. He was able to bring relatively minor matters to Parliament's attention. He arranged for a private Member's Bill which gave women police officers full voting rights in the Federation; and it was through his efforts that the Police Act was amended so as to alter the date of the Federation's annual conference. More importantly, he played a major part in the negotiations which led to the setting up of a Royal Commission on the Police, in 1960. In 1964 Mr Callaghan became Chancellor of the Exchequer in the Labour government elected to office that year. At first the Federation considered it had no need of a successor to him. But the amount of parliamentary activity affecting police officers – especially the controversy surrounding the campaign to abolish the death penalty for murder – seems to have convinced it otherwise. Just before the 1966 general election the Federation appointed a new Consultant, the Conservative MP for Bury St Edmunds, Eldon Griffiths, the son of a Lancashire policeman (A. Judge, 1968).

It would be wrong to regard Mr Callaghan or Mr Griffiths as 'spokesmen' for the Federation. Nonetheless, the knowledge that the Federation has at least one senior and well-respected MP to whom it can turn for advice is clearly of considerable benefit, particularly in regard to matters which transcend party political divisions. But the forging of special links and contractual relationships with MPs are by no means the only methods available to pressure groups which seek to make their voice heard at the Palace of Westminster. Many of the 'all-party' committees set up within Parliament are actually serviced by outside groups; such committees could not function without the assistance of the groups, which provide the money, expertise, secretarial and research facilities of which Parliament itself has always been so short.

The constitution and working of the Parliamentary and Scientific Committee provide the precedent and model for such activities. The PASC describes itself as 'an unofficial group of members of both Houses of Parliament and British members of the European Parliament and representatives of certain scientific and technical institutions and some science-based companies'. It was formed in November 1939 on the initiative of the Labour MP Frank Markham, who invited Commander Christopher Powell to provide the PASC with a secretariat. Commander Powell was then a partner in the firm of parliamentary consultants known as Watney & Powell (now Charles Barker, Watney & Powell), and he became the Committee's Administrative Secretary; the firm still provides the secretariat, which is paid for out of subscriptions collected from individual and corporate members.

The PASC's title was formally approved by the Clerk of the House of Commons in March 1943. Although, therefore, the Committee is not *of* the House of Commons or *of* the House of Lords, it has links with Parliament which are, to all intents and purposes, formal and officially recognized. Its membership is drawn on the one hand from scientific and technical organizations, and on the other from MPs and peers; in 1981 79 peers, 140 MPs and 34 Members of the European Parliament were PASC members, together with representatives of 158 scientific bodies. These scientific and technical members include most of the leading industrial and technological organizations to be found operating in the United Kingdom today, from the Royal Society and the British Association for the Advancement of Science to the Society of Cosmetic Chemists and the Water Research Centre. In addition, there were in 1981 no less than 62 associate-member companies and undertakings, including such industrial giants as the Beecham Group, the Distillers Company, Imperial Chemical Industries and Tube Investments (Powell and Butler 1980:92–102). Parliamentary members in 1981 included the Prime Minister and many leading backbenchers from the major parties.

The aims of the PASC, as enumerated in its *Annual Report* for 1981, include the following:

1. To provide Members of Parliament with authoritative scientific information from time to time in connection with debates.
2. To bring to the notice of Members of Parliament and Government Departments the results of scientific research and technological developments which bear upon questions of current public interest.
3. To arrange for suitable action through Parliamentary channels whenever necessary to ensure that proper regard is had for the scientific point of view.
4. To examine all legislation likely to affect the above and take such action as may be suitable.
5. To watch the financing of scientific and technological research, education and development.
6. To provide its members and other approved Subscribers with a regular summary of scientific matters dealt with in Parliament.

Within these broad headings the activities of the PASC include regular monthly discussion meetings at the House of Commons; discussion dinners, visits to research establishments and industrial undertakings; an annual lunch; and the setting up, from time to time, of investigative sub-committees. In 1964 one such subcommittee was established to consider improving access by MPs to scientific information concerning matters before Parliament; representations were made to the House of Commons' Library and, as a result, the Library established a Scientific Unit within its Research Division.

Thus far the PASC might be regarded as an extremely useful nonpartisan body from which, over the years, Parliament and the nation have derived considerable benefit: a forum where politicians and scientists can meet on equal terms. But among the procedures adopted by the PASC the following *modus operandi* is listed (Powell and Butler 1980:14).

> Encouragement of suitable action in the parliamentary sphere by MPs and peers in membership of the Committee, in conjunction with debates, legislation and so forth.

What does this 'encouragement of suitable action in the parliamentary sphere' mean in practice? The authors of the PASC's official history admit that 'the main value of the Parliamentary and Scientific Committee . . . has been to exert a continuing influence over Parliament and government'. And it is undeniable that over the years the Committee has acted as a powerful but subtle pressure group on behalf of science-based industry. In January 1979, for example, the PASC sponsored a seminar at the House of Commons to discuss the Common Market's draft directive on product liability and the report of the Royal Commission on Civil Liability and Compensation for Personal Injury (the Pearson Report). The seminar was opened by none other than the Secretary of State for Prices and Consumer Protection, Roy Hattersley, who acknowledged industrial concern about the proposals on product liability and promised that the views of affected parties would be given serious consideration. In July 1979 Mr Hattersley's Conservative successor, Mrs Sally Oppenheim, received a deputation from the PASC which urged that producers should not have to bear the whole of the responsibility for compensation caused by defective products. In the event, the government rejected the major legislative change then being urged by consumer groups, the extension of the strict liability of producers (Powell and Butler 1980:43–5). The PASC can thus rightly claim to have played a central part in this assault on the Pearson recommendations.

Therefore, although the PASC provides an invaluable service to MPs and peers interested in scientific and technological matters, it also manages to behave as an avenue through which science-based industries can influence parliamentary and government proceedings (Walkland 1964). With the mushrooming of all-party committees since 1945, the opportunities for pressure-group activity along these lines have grown considerably. In the 1970–71 parliamentary session there were nine such committees dealing with social and welfare issues, eleven in the fields of technology, trade and industry, four environmental groups and a miscellany of other *ad hoc* committees.

On the one hand they provide MPs with specialist information they would find exceedingly difficult to obtain elsewhere. On the other, they persuade MPs to table questions and to put down Early Day motions in order to publicise their views (D. Judge 1981:142). In other ways, too, they act as mouthpieces for extra-parliamentary organizations. The Animal Welfare Group gives voice to the policies of the Royal Society for the Prevention of Cruelty to Animals; the British Limbless Ex-Servicemen's Association has an all-party committee to act for it.

Sometimes, indeed, a pressure group has been known to sponsor the creation of an all-party committee. The Council for Nature played a central role in the formation of the all-party Committee for the Conservation of Species and Habitats (Brookes and Richardson 1975:324). It is certainly the case that all-party committees are capable of exerting a major influence upon public policy. During the parliament of 1970–74 the Disablement Committee worked strenuously to bring disablement matters to Parliament's attention, and was closely involved in the passage of the 1970 Chronically Sick and Disabled Persons Act (D. Judge 1981:143). The activities of the all-party Third London Airport Committee, formed after the 1970 general election, were vital to the success of the campaign to convince the government that the airport should not be built at Wing. The committee arranged meetings with and visits by MPs; it issued press releases; organized backbench opposition to the idea of an inland site; and stage-managed parliamentary debate on the issue. Richardson and Kimber (1972:347) conclude that

> Whatever the Government's reasons for choosing Foulness, the committee, by demonstrating considerable cross-bench opposition to an inland site, together with the massive extra-parliamentary campaign waged by WARA [Wing Airport Resistance Association] managed to effectively close off one of the Government's main options.

But the relationship between organized groups and all-party committees goes deeper than this. Like the PASC, many other all-party committees of MPs are actually serviced by pressure groups. The National Association for Mental Health (MIND) provides secretarial and administrative services for the all-party committee on mental health; Age Concern provides similar assistance for the committee on pensions, as does the National Association for the Care and Resettlement of Offenders in relation to the all-party committee on Penal Affairs; the committee on smoking is serviced by Action on Smoking and Health (Bradley 9 Apr. 1980:2). Such servicing activities give the groups unique opportunities to feed the parliamentary system with the 'right' reports and the 'right' policy documents. They also provide opportunities for groups to use the name and facilities of Parliament, and to claim the authority of the all-party committees they service for the extra-parliamentary campaigns they wage.

All-party committees must of course be distinguished from Select and Standing Committees. The latter are official committees of Parliament to inquire into certain matters or to examine legislation in detail after the second-reading stage; the all-party committees are in reality 'clubs' of parliamentarians with common interests. But we might note that some Standing Committees are prone to pressure-group influence in exactly the same way as all-party committees. Some pressure groups go out of their way to form friendly relationships with MPs serving on Standing Committees, in order to try to obtain amendments to Bills and to be informed about the government's (or the opposition's) intentions. Contacts with opposition MPs can be especially important. Professor Griffith (1981:124–5) writes,

> On important bills the affected interests outside Parliament will be anxious to help in the hope of bringing further pressure to bear on the Government to accept amendments. And if they are powerful they will be well and expertly staffed and will have or will engage lawyers to draft amendments so that all Opposition members need to do, if they are so minded, is to sign the amendment provided and hand it in to the Public Bill Office. At times, this servicing by professionals and experts comes close in its drafting and in its briefing to the service provided for the Minister by his department.

Thus in 1980, during the passage of the Social Security Bill, the Labour MPs who were members of the Standing Committee dealing with the Bill invited a number of interested pressure groups to attend their weekly briefing meetings and help with the drafting of amendments. A much more blatant case is provided by the history of the passage of the Education Act of 1981. This Act arose out of the Warnock Report on the education of mentally and physically handicapped children, who of necessity have special educational needs. When the Bill was presented, it omitted any reference to a central recommendation of the Warnock Report, that there should be a 'named person' to whom parents of such children could turn for support, guidance and advice. During the Standing Committee stage an amendment with the object of carrying out this recommendation was tabled by a Conservative member of the Committee, John Hannam. Since the Conservative government had a majority of only one on this particular Standing Committee, it was obliged to accept the amendment, which was thus carried into law. But in fact the amendment had been drafted by the research assistant to the all-party Disablement Committee, consisting of about seventy-five MPs and peers. Mr Hannam, a Member of Parliament well-known for his work on behalf of the disabled, was chairman of this Committee, and the research assistant's salary was paid by one of the large disability associations.*

The 1981 Education Act was admittedly out of the ordinary. It was a non-party measure and its relatively easy passage was assured by a great deal of goodwill from all sides in Parliament. It did not commit the government to make any new resources available. It aroused no parliamentary opposition. The Warnock Report, out of which it grew, had itself been prompted by the publicity given to children with special educational needs by a variety of pressure groups, such as MENCAP. The unique contribution of the voluntary societies to the problems of these children, and the societies' unrivalled expertise in this area, were universally acknowledged, and the government rightly accorded them a healthy respect. So it was natural that they should take a detailed interest in the passage of the Bill. But the role of the relevant all-party group was not untypical. It acted, from the purest of motives, as a means by which pressure groups were able to take part more or less directly in the legislative work of Parliament.

What of those groups that can find no sympathetic MP to support them, and for which there exists no all-party committee conveniently to hand? Such groups may well feel that they have no alternative but to take their campaigns beyond the confines of Westminster, perhaps by organizing a 'lobby' of Parliament as part of a wider spectrum of largely extra-parliamentary activities of publicity and pressure; such activities will be considered in Chapter 5. Or they may feel that their best approach lies in developing contacts with central government, thus by-passing the legislature altogether; this aspect will be considered in Chapter 4. But if they still wish to exert influence *within* Westminster, one further avenue lies open to them: they might consider employing a broker, or agent, to supplicate and intercede with the politicians on their behalf.

A number of the wealthier pressure groups do of course employ, perhaps full-time, an official or officials whose business it is to main-

* The origin of this amendment was revealed in a BBC radio programme, 'In On The Act', broadcast in November 1981 and presented by Antony Barker.

tain and develop contacts with MPs, and generally to keep an eye on parliamentary developments. The Spastics Society, for example, employs a 'Lobbyist', responsible to its Director, whose job it is to maintain 'close contact with a large number of Members of Parliament, Civil servants, and other public officials' (*The Guardian*, 30 Sept. 1981:17). *The Times* of 21 January 1982 carried an advertisement for a 'Parliamentary Affairs Officer' to be appointed to an 'Expanding [but unnamed] Major British Professional Institute'. Applicants were required to have had 'a minimum of 4 years practical experience of the political and parliamentary process at Westminster', and the responsibilities of the post were declared to be 'the maintenance of formal and informal contact with members of both Houses of Parliament and Civil Servants, the provision of briefings on subjects of material interest to the Institute, the monitoring of Parliamentary proceedings and assistance with research and speech writing'. The salary (a maximum of £15,500 p.a. plus many fringe benefits) compared favourably with salaries of MPs and senior civil servants.

Often, duties such as these are part of a wider 'public relations' role. But whether or not a pressure group has such an employee on its payroll, it may well decide to engage the services of an outside professional parliamentary agent or consultant. Located inconspicuously around the Palace of Westminster, in Great College Street, Tothill Street or The Sanctuary, are to be found the offices of eight long-established legal firms who style themselves and are authorized to practise as 'parliamentary agents'. They are solicitors specializing in parliamentary work, much of which is concerned with drafting private Bills on behalf of clients, and piloting such Bills through the intricate private Bill procedure of both Houses of Parliament. Their clients range from large corporations, such as the British Railways Board and many local authorities, to humble individuals; in 1981 a step-father and his step-daughter successfully promoted a private Bill to allow them to marry in spite of the general prohibition on such marriages in English law.

Naturally, parliamentary agents are also retained by those who oppose the passage of particular private Bills, or who object to certain clauses in them; in this way an agent may well find himself bargaining on behalf of his client with a fellow agent acting for the other side. Just occasionally, parliamentary agents are retained by backbench MPs to draft amendments or perhaps whole Bills. In that case, it is likely that a vested interest outside Parliament will have put up the money to finance the operation. Dr Eric Taylor, the Clerk in Charge of Committee Records at the House of Commons, has recorded that during the passage of the Parliament No.2 Bill of 1969 (which attempted unsuccessfully to reform the House of Lords) at least one MP engaged a private firm to research into the subject and provide him with material which he used to good effect during the Bill's committee stage (Taylor 1971:98). Such work is, in Dr Taylor's words, 'a profitable addition' to the normal duties of parliamentary agents, who may well, in this manner, find themselves acting on behalf of pressure groups. But these agents are not public relations consultants. They do not undertake campaigns.

The parliamentary consultant sees his role very differently. He undertakes to mount entire campaigns on behalf of his clients, in much the same way as advertising agents plan and execute campaigns in the press and on radio and television. But whereas an advertising agent or a public relations firm will mount such a campaign in a very public manner, the parliamentary consultant goes about his business with the utmost discretion, and usually with a great deal of secrecy. His job is to develop, on behalf of his client, contacts at the highest governmental levels, both at Westminster and in Whitehall. This may involve sumptuous lunches and dinner-parties, perhaps (through the good offices of a friendly MP) in the dining rooms of the Houses of Parliament, as well as sponsored visits, even trips abroad. Because of the confidential nature of much of this work, it is impossible to form a comprehensive assessment of the political impact of parliamentary consultants. Nonetheless it is possible to gain some insight, admittedly partial, into the way such consultants operate and the scope of their activities.

The pioneer in this type of work appears to have been Commander Powell, mentioned earlier, who formed a partnership with the late Charles Watney in 1928 in order to provide 'parliamentary consultancy, information and secretarial services' (Powell and Butler 1980:11). Today there are perhaps as many as twenty companies operating in these fields. Charles Barker Lyons Ltd, the parent company of Charles Barker Watney & Powell, is by far the largest of them; in 1981 its annual fee income was over £1 million, it was retained by over 170 different organizations and acted for fifty-nine others. Its clientele range from the Equipment Leasing Association and the Association of Optical Practitioners to the Institute of Professional Civil Servants and the Research Defence Society; the clientele includes several all-party committees, for which the company apparently provides the secretariats.

Another firm of parliamentary consultants, Lloyd-Hughes

Associates, claims to offer 'unrivalled links with and insights into the corridors of power', and declares that it has 'master-minded' parliamentary campaigns and has inspired parliamentary questions by MPs in order to 'obtain information for our clients' (quoted in Hetherington 1981:670). The company is understandably reticent about its work; a letter of enquiry sent by the present author has remained unanswered. In February 1982, however, one of its brochures was accorded the rare privilege of extensive quotation in Hansard (HC *Debates*, 2 Feb. 1982: cols 127–8):

> Our success [the brochure declaimed] derives from confidence that we can match promise with performance. Notable specific successes have been achieved. Among them, we have saved the international motor-car and motor cycle industries based in the United Kingdom millions of pounds by persuading the Government to exempt them from the provisions of the Trade Descriptions Act, severely reduced demands on an American company for back-payments of British excise duties, secured British Government planning permission for an oil platform building site.

The brochure further boasts that Lloyd-Hughes Associates have 'arranged for business leaders, including the heads of American and French as well as British companies, to have private meetings with eminent personalities in London, including Cabinet Ministers ... the Queen's principal private secretary, former British Ambassadors, and men at the very top of the United Kingdom Diplomatic and Home Civil Services'. And the brochure adds ominously:

> We normally expect to achieve results without any publicity. But, on occasion, even Ministers and senior officials have asked us to help in creating a particular climate of public opinion to enable them the more easily to assist one of our clients whose case they have accepted.

Another firm, Camden Consultants, mounted a successful campaign on behalf of the Pools Promoters Association, which was anxious to prevent the implementation of a Royal Commission recommendation that 'spot the ball' competitions should be made illegal. Camden Consultants made contact with a number of MPs, and arranged for them to take part in presentations to football clubs of moneys derived from these competitions; the government subsequently agreed the competitions should be reprieved (Hetherington 1981:670). A third firm of parliamentary consultants was engaged by members of the electrical trade who wished to quash regulations which had already been laid before Parliament, and which would have required costly changes in the design of the standard electric light socket. The grounds for quashing the regulations were substantial: there had been very few accidents with existing sockets, and the change would have necessitated an expenditure of many millions of pounds in retooling. The case of the electrical industry was put to a dozen MPs; then the Minister was approached informally, and told that he could expect trouble in Parliament if the regulations were not withdrawn. They were (Hetherington 1981:671).

In yet another case, the firm of parliamentary consultants known as Political Research & Communication International was instrumental in fostering the organization of the Take Away & Fast Food Federation and was successful in preventing the Greater London Council, in 1976, from acquiring the legal authority to compel 'take away' food establishments to close at 11.00 p.m. each evening; Parliament accepted the argument put forward by the firm that such a move would have seriously damaged the tourist industry in the nation's capital (Hoggart 1978). Another company, David McDonagh and Associates Ltd., appears to specialize in the 'working lunch concept', 'an effective weapon', it explains to potential clients, 'in your corporate communications armoury'. This firm will 'recommend a suitable place' for such a lunch – 'an hotel, restaurant or club; or perhaps, in appropriate circumstances, the House of Commons' (HC *Debates*, 2 Feb. 1982: col.128).

There is nothing at all improper in the work parliamentary consultants perform. The Pools Promoters Association, or the electrical trade, could have approached individual MPs themselves, or obtained the services of MPs in exactly the same way as the Police Federation or the National Association of Bookmakers. But which MPs should one approach? The parliamentary consultant knows precisely which ones to contact, and in what manner. There are certainly grounds (discussed in the final chapter) for making more information publicly available about parliamentary consultants and their work and clients. But it is important to remember that, so far as Parliament is concerned, they cannot go further than MPs whom they approach are willing to be taken. In 1982 the Labour MP Robert Cryer argued in the Commons that 'the brochures [of parliamentary consultants] suggests that some of the lobbyists are treading the narrow line which can exist between proper representations put forward with excessive zeal and the subversion of the democratic process' (HC *Debates*, 2 Feb. 1982: col.129). He instanced a brochure put out by Charles Barker Watney & Powell which displayed, on its front cover, the official portcullis crest of the Palace of Westminster; this emblem had been removed after complaint.

Behaviour of this sort certainly cannot be condoned; but it does not amount to a subversion of the democratic process. If parliamentary consultants ever do subvert democracy, this can only be because politicians and civil servants allow themselves to become willing participants in the subversion process.

Chapter four
PRESSURE GROUPS AND THE ADMINISTRATION

During the nineteenth century, pressure groups favoured action through Parliament, for it was at Westminster that the domestic affairs of the nation were decided. In the twentieth century, and for the reasons set down in the first chapter, the central arena of decision-making in British government has moved to Whitehall, to the bureaucrats in the great departments of state. When a government has a secure parliamentary majority it can count on getting most if not all of its legislative proposals onto the statute book. Legislation is drafted in government departments. So it is natural that pressure groups affected by proposed legislation should be as concerned with these departments as with the Houses of Parliament. But central government also possesses ever wider authority not merely of administration, of enforcing the laws, but of executive action, by delegation of powers. At the same time, in a liberal democracy it is essential for the smooth functioning of government that the consent of interested parties be obtained both to the laws that it is proposed to enact and to the manner in which those laws, once enacted, are applied. Pressure groups are therefore much interested in obtaining access to the bureaucracy which draws up and enforces the laws. Equally, the bureaucracy has an interest in maintaining a dialogue with those groups without which there cannot be good government. In this way it is possible for some groups to become themselves part of the machinery of government. Where no pressure group exists, British governments have been known to create one, in order to facilitate the mobilization of consent, or to foster the impression of dialogue, or perhaps to form a buffer between central government and the masses. For some groups, pushing a foot into the corridors of Whitehall is the hardest of tasks. But for others the invitation to walk those corridors is gilt-edged, and delivered by hand.

Whereas the relationship between individual MPs and pressure groups, and the political role of these groups, have given rise to a great deal of public concern, much less anxiety seems to have been aroused by the relationship between pressure groups and central government, including individual civil servants. Groups which retain MPs on their payroll, or which sponsor MPs or make payments to them, have been accused of undermining representative government in this country. But the close relationship between some groups and certain government departments has generally gone unremarked. This is partly because of the persistent conviction that governments propose but Parliament decides, a conviction which few MPs hold and which flies in the face of the evidence (Richardson and Jordan 1979). It is also based on the fiction that the British civil servant really is an unbiased neutral administrator, bound to follow the dictates of his political master.

In examining the role of pressure groups in relation to the central administration, therefore, we might begin by looking at the duties and obligations of civil servants. Contacts between pressure groups and civil servants are facilitated by the conspiracy of silence and secrecy which surrounds many of the activities of civil servants. The degree of silence and secrecy seems to depend entirely on the whim of individual departmental officers. In the course of researching this book the author approached government departments with requests for non-attributable interviews with senior government advisers. A senior civil servant at the Department of Education and Science not only gave such an interview but proved extremely helpful in other ways. The Home Office, by contrast, refused the request on the grounds that 'it is a general rule that a civil servant is not permitted to take part in a survey or similar project if the subject matter is connected with his official duties'. Chapter and verse for this rule were nowhere stated; the so-called 'rule' appears all the more astonishing in view of the fact that, eighteen months previously, the author had himself been invited to present to the Home Office a report on a matter then under consideration, and had been asked to meet, at the Home Office, a civil servant dealing with this matter. It seems that the Home Office did not wish its staff to be interviewed about the relationship between the department and pressure groups, and was determined that such interviews should not take place.

Civil servants know that they are expected to consult all persons and organizations having an interest in a particular area of government policy. Many contacts between civil servants and interested parties are initiated at face-to-face meetings or by telephone conversations; formal letters and conferences come later. Civil servants are not obliged to divulge the nature of these contacts to Parliament or the public. Indeed, the *Memorandum of Guidance for Officials Appearing before Select Committees*, issued by the Civil Service Department on 16 May 1980, authorizes the withholding of information by government officials 'in the interests of good government' (p. 5). The definition of 'good government' is left to the individual civil servant to determine. The *Memorandum* (pp. 7–8) also prohibits government officials from revealing the advice given to Ministers by their departments; information about interdepartmental exchanges on policy issues; questions 'in the field of political controversy'; sensitive information of a commercial or economic nature; and what are termed 'matters which are, or may become the subject of sensitive negotiations with Governments or other bodies'. Where a Select Committee calls for evidence from a non-departmental body (such as a nationalized industry) for which a government department has responsibility, the *Memorandum* encourages the department to discuss the evidence with the appropriate witnesses before the Committee hearing.

When appearing before Select Committees, therefore, there is plenty of authority for civil servants to say precisely nothing about the contacts with pressure groups which have led to a particular departmental decision, or course of governmental action. Even when such information is given, it need not be complete 'in the interests of good government'. These guidelines also apply to press releases and other contacts with the public. The ability of backbench MPs to probe the relationship between a department of state and a pressure group by means of parliamentary questions is also severely restricted. The list of 'prohibited subjects' is long, and includes such matters as confidential details of research contracts; forecasts of changes in food prices; education matters which would involve a breach of confidence; and individual applications for industrial development certificates (*The Times*, 4 May 1978:4).

It is also worth recording that the official *Civil Service Pay and Conditions Code*, also issued in May 1980, warns those officials who advise Ministers and who carry out Ministers' policies, that 'they should not normally take an active part in any matter which is or could be one of public or political controversy whether or not it is one with which they are officially concerned' (para. 9870(e)). Since the anonymity of civil servants is protected by the doctrine of ministerial responsibility, it is thus possible for a great deal of contact with pressure groups to take place in complete secrecy. Although there are, of course, very strict rules, emanating from the Prevention of Corruption Acts of 1906 and 1916, prohibiting the acceptance by a government officer of any gift or consideration as an inducement or reward to do, or refrain from doing, anything in his official capacity, it is recognized that 'conventional hospitality' may be accepted. And there is, specifically, 'no objection to the acceptance of, for example, an invitation to the annual dinner of a large trade association or similar body with which a department is much in day to day contact; or of working lunches (provided the frequency is reasonable) in the course of official visits' (*Code*, para. 9882).

These strictures and permissions form the ground-rules within which pressure groups and government departments operate and work together. The operational requirements of modern British government oblige civil servants to take *some* pressure groups into their confidence, for without the willing assistance of these groups whole areas of government activity would grind to a halt. Exactly *which* groups are consulted, or are regarded as having a 'proper' interest in a particular matter, is entirely for the civil servants to determine. There seem to be no fixed rules or standard procedures by which departmental officials make their choice. Some are very careful to check the credentials of a group, and to insist on examining its constitution and internal government. Others rely on third-party reports (usually recommendations from those they already know) or from the private secretaries of Ministers. Others go by the public standing of the office-holders, which is why a peer or two among the 'honorary vice-presidents' is always a good plan. Different civil servants within the same department of state have different ways of approaching these problems.

We may now identify three areas within which such co-operation between pressure groups and civil servants is, from the point of view of central government, essential: the formulation and execution of policy; the staffing and operation of government agencies; and the provision of information. We may also identify a fourth area, the legitimation of government policy, where such co-operation, though not essential, is highly desirable and may carry a political importance of its own.

Information is the raw material of the governing process. Surprisingly, perhaps, British governments possess very little information of their own; and most of that relates to bare statistical data. A table showing the incidence of foot-and-mouth disease in cattle is not an answer to the question 'how can the disease be prevented or, if an outbreak occurs, how can it best be contained?'. A print-out of successful prosecutions for offences against the Sunday trading laws is not a policy document for the regulations of Sunday trading. A school-by-school list of the numbers of children taking CSE and 'O' Level General Certificate of Education examinations is not the starting point for an education policy. This type of data, which British civil servants are good at collecting, must be interpreted and evaluated. But, except in the Scientific Civil Service, there is no tradition of concentrated expertise in British central government. The tradition, for better or worse, has been that administrators go to those *outside* government, who are considered to have the necessary expertise to advise on policy alternatives. This is cheaper than retaining, permanently, experts in all fields of government activity; it also gives opportunities for those outside government to become involved in central administration. It may not be the most efficient way of running a country; probably it isn't. But it is a most important component of the notion of government by consent, and it requires the constant co-operation of pressure groups if it is to work at all.

How is the advice obtained? Primarily through advisory committees, some with the grandiose title of Royal Commissions, others known simply as working parties, some permanent and some *ad hoc*. The exact number of these committees has never been determined. In 1958 it appears there were about 850 (HC *Debates*, 20 Nov 1958: col.1305). On 20 October 1976, in answer to a parliamentary question from the Conservative MP David Knox, it was revealed that the Lord Chancellor alone was advised by at least 250 advisory committees on Justices of the Peace in England and Wales and 78 advisory committees on General Commissioners of Income Tax. Although many of these advisory bodies are staffed by civil servants, substantial proportions of their memberships are provided by outside groups, and some of them, such as the British National Export Council and the White Fish Authority Research and Development Committee, are run jointly by government departments and outside groups (Hague, Mackenzie and Barker 1975:411).

In general, the joint responsibility thus created seems to be welcomed by the groups concerned. Representation upon an advisory committee is a way of expressing views to the government, and to other groups, and affords an insurance against interests being left undefended. Such representation is, moreover, devoid of any financial commitment (Political and Economic Planning 1960:91). It is also a status symbol. But joint responsibility does impose an obligation. For it is not only an administrative burden which is shared, but an executive one as well, allowing the government to shed (to some extent) culpability at times of adverse criticism. The administration of education policy in Britain provides many examples to illustrate this point. The Central Advisory Councils for Education, set up in England and Wales under the 1944 Education Act, were used by the Department of Education and Science as a means of scrutinizing departmental policies, but also as a machinery for conducting negotiations within the education services (Kogan and Packwood 1974: 82–5). In 1973 the Department set up 'ACSET', the Advisory Committee on the Supply and Education of Teachers. ACSET deliberates on the matters within its purview, and it publishes reports. Its membership includes representatives from the University Grants Committee, the Association of University Teachers, and the National Association of Teachers in Further and Higher Education. But one of its purposes, as expressed candidly by an official of the Department, is to 'draw the teeth' of the teaching unions; perhaps for this reason the National Union of Teachers has refused to become part of it.

Inevitably, there is a grey area where the 'giving of advice' and the 'taking of decisions' meet. Jordan and Richardson, in their study of the Central Advisory Water Committee, set up under the provisions of the 1945 Water Act, demonstrate that though members were appointed to this committee as individuals, in fact they 'represented' 'parent' groups, which were thus able to make a contribution to general policy discussion on the use of water resources (Jordan and Richardson 1977:46). But a more blatant example is provided by the relationship between the Ministry of Agriculture and the National Farmers' Union. The Ministry is heavily dependent upon the Farmers' Union for membership of several dozen agricultural advisory committees. The formal basis of this relationship is the 1947 Agriculture Act, which sought to achieve a balance between 'security' for the agriculture industry and 'efficiency'. The major bulwark of security is the Annual Price Review, at which the level of guaranteed prices and subsidies for the coming year is determined. The main instruments of agricultural efficiency are the County Agricultural Committees, which possess powers of supervision and dispossession, and which administer many subsidies and regulations. Three members of each County Agricultural Committee are selected from nominations made by the National Farmers' Union; but in practice the number of Union members on each Committee is often much greater. In addition, the Union has been granted automatic representation on a wide range of agricultural bodies, such as the Hill Farming Advisory Committee, the Myxomatosis Advisory Committee and the Bee Diseases Advisory Committee. It is no exaggeration to say that, without the willing co-operation of the National Farmers' Union, the implementation, and, most probably, the formulation, of agricultural policy in Britain would simply not be possible (Self and Storing 1974:67–6).

Clearly, if the advice of an advisory committee subsequently becomes government policy, groups represented (*de jure* or *de facto*) on that committee may in truth be said to have taken a government decision themselves. In that case the advisory committee may be a convenient shield behind which certain pressure groups constitute themselves as executive boards to help govern the country. Occasionally even this facade is dispensed with, and pressure groups are formally given the task of decision-making. Historically, the area of public administration in which this tradition is best known is that concerned with the preparation of delegated legislation. It is unthinkable that a Minister of the Crown would deliberately proceed to make rules without consulting at least the most important of the interests involved: the Law Society in relation to the regulation of solicitors; the British Medical Association in relation to general practitioners; the local government associations in relation to local authorities; and so on.

Sometimes there is a statutory requirement to consult with specified interests. The Food and Drugs Act of 1956 required Ministers to consult with such organizations as appeared to them to be representative of interests substantially affected by regulations to be made under the Act. Thus, before making the Food Standards (Ice Cream) Regulations of 1959, thirty-one organizations were consulted, including local authority associations, public analysts, public health inspectors, the Milk Marketing Board, ice-cream manufacturers' associations, the United Synagogue, the British Diabetic Association and the British Standards Institution (HC *Debates*, 17 July 1958: cols 1419–20). Under the 1965 National Insurance Act (sect. 108), regulations relating to the national insurance scheme must be submitted to the National Insurance Advisory Committee and this Committee must, in turn, advertise the proposed regulations and consider any objections to them; the Committee's report must be laid before Parliament. The Protection of Birds Act, 1954 (sect 13) imposes an obligation upon the Home Secretary to consult an advisory committee before making any order for the protection of birds; representatives of relevant animal welfare organizations are (in fact if not in theory) members of this advisory committee.

Should a Minister fail to consult an interest which he clearly ought to have consulted, it may be that the interest so ignored, or overlooked, will not be bound by subsequent legislation. In one case which came to court in 1972 a government Minister was under an obligation, before making an industrial training order, to consult associations which appeared to him to be representative of those concerned. Many organizations were, therefore, invited to give their views about a proposed order for the agricultural industries; but a letter sent to the mushroom growers' association was lost, and that association was consequently not consulted. It was held that members of the association were not bound by the order, because a mandatory requirement had not been observed (Wade 1977:718).

Much more extraordinary, however, is the delegation, by statute, of the power to *draft* a statutory instrument to a representative group: the Minister is relegated to the role of a confirming or approving authority. Under the Cereals Marketing Act of 1965 the Home-Grown Cereals Authority was given power to prepare and submit schemes to the appropriate Ministers for their approval (Griffith and Street 1967:131). It is true that the power to approve still rests with the Crown and – ultimately – with Parliament. Nonetheless the practical effect is to endow the groups represented on the Authority with real legislative ability.

But, quite apart from the special case of subordinate legislation, governments seem readier than ever to devolve responsibility to pressure groups. The events which led to the setting up of Motability, an 'independent' organization established in 1977 to provide specially adapted cars for disabled drivers, demonstrates in a remarkable way how governments can approach pressure groups to help solve problems they cannot or are unwilling to solve themselves. Briefly, until the late 1940s disabled people who wished to drive had to make their own financial provision; there was no government help. Then a scheme was introduced which, in time, provided three-wheeled motorized invalid carriages. However, during the early 1970s serious criticisms were levelled against these 'trikes' on grounds of safety. The Labour government accepted that the trikes were dangerous and decided to cease providing them; instead, a mobility allowance was instituted, which by the end of 1977 stood at £7 per week. This was nowhere near enough to enable disabled drivers to replace their trikes with specially converted cars.

The government was not prepared to find the money to provide such cars itself. At the same time it faced considerable criticism from disabled groups who, with their parliamentary friends, argued that there was a moral obligation on the government to achieve a satisfactory solution to this question. The Minister of State at the Department of Health, David Ennals, approached Lord Goodman, who was asked to use his influence in the City to help set up a scheme which would convert the mobility allowance into cars; trade unions and voluntary organizations dealing with the disabled were drawn into the discussions. The outcome was Motability, a voluntary charity run by a civil servant seconded from the Department. With capital raised from the clearing banks, Motability is able to arrange with appropriate suppliers for cars to be leased to disabled drivers, who agree, in return, to have their weekly mobility allowance paid directly to Motability Finance (*The Times*, 28 Dec. 1981:8).

The administrative advantage to the government here is very clear. It has no responsibility for the decisions Motability makes; on the contrary, the charity it has set up acts as a buffer between the Department of Health and the voluntary bodies which speak on behalf of disabled people. It is also certain that the administration of the scheme by a charity, in the establishment of which the relevant representative groups have had a say, is much more acceptable – and politically safer – than a scheme run by the government alone. It is partly for this reason that governments recognize that under certain circumstances such groups are better able to carry out policy decisions. These groups may also have broader and more pervasive local knowledge than centrally-located officials. There is another factor. Government officials must be paid. Government by pressure group is a cheap way of running, if not the entire country, then at least certain often important areas of public administration. And governments have been known to admit that organized groups sometimes provide a service which Whitehall cannot hope to match.

Motability is a clear example of a body deliberately created by the Government with the help of representative groups. But it is by no means an isolated case. In November 1945 the President of the Board of Trade appointed a committee 'to formulate detailed proposals for setting up a central Institute for all questions connected with management', in order to promote the efficient development of post-war industry. The committee recommended a central organization to be called the British Institute of Management which, financed partly by the Exchequer, was established in 1945; it merged with the Institute of Industrial Administration in 1951 (Millerson 1964:73).

Some more recent examples of officially-inspired pressure groups are provided by the developing policy of the Department of Education towards a national youth service. In the mid-1970s the British Youth Council, then dominated by the National Union of Students, claimed to be the authoritative voice of British youth and, on that basis, asked for public money to finance its activities. The Department of Education was naturally suspicious and, for a time, resisted these approaches. But it became clear that while the existing National Council for Voluntary Youth Services was regarded with suspicion by young people, the British Youth Council continued to attract support. The government needed a 'consultative interface' with the youth service; it was evident that only the British Youth Council was capable of meeting this requirement. So there was a change of policy. The Department of Education investigated the British Youth Council's constitution, which was amended on agreed lines. Taxpayers' money was then made available to it. A 'major consideration' (the phrase is that of a senior civil servant who dealt with this matter), both in relation to this affair and to the foundation of the Youth Service Development Council, created by the Department at Leicester in 1973 as a 'mainstream' youth club movement, was to 'shift the blame', to facilitate the provision of government finance to the youth service, while at the same time distancing the government from the policy decisions taken in regard to the spending of that financial provision and the consequences that might flow therefrom.

More generally, we may note that grants by central and local government to pressure groups are now commonplace. The Keep Britain Tidy group, an anti-litter organization, receives an annual grant from the Department of the Environment. The National Council of Social Service is also in receipt of public money (Richardson and Jordan 1979:149). The National Council on Alcoholism and the Alcohol Education Centre, together with other bodies active in the field of alcohol misuse and abuse, received in 1982 grants from the Department of Health totalling £300,000 (*The Times*, 22 Apr. 1982:4). Action on Smoking and Health, established under the auspices of the Royal College of Physicians in 1971, now also receives a grant from the Department of Health; one government department thus subsidizes an organization whose activities are designed to reduce the revenue to another government department, the Exchequer. In 1981 a number of mental health organizations, including MENCAP and MIND, received grants in excess of £200,000 (*The Times*, 13 Feb. 1982:3). The following year the Family Fund, which caters for the needs of families with severely handicapped children, received a government subvention of £4.6 millions (*The Times*, 6 Mar. 1982:3).

Sometimes, governments are *obliged* to fund pressure groups, because to refuse to do so would attract very unwelcome publicity. The case of the National Society for the Prevention of Cruelty to Children has already been mentioned (see Chap. 2). In January 1982 the Secretary of State for Social Services, Norman Fowler, announced that the Society would receive grants totalling £450,000 for the period down to April 1984. Without these grants, *The Times* declared (16 Jan. 1982:3), 'services might be cut and children would almost certainly die'. In 1978–9 the Society had received £125,000 in government aid, and a further £100,000 the following year; but until 1982 it had never received grants on a long-term basis. Before the 1982–4 grants were announced there had been a careful publicity campaign, timed to coincide with a visit to the Society's London office by Lord Elton, the Under-Secretary of State; the two-year grant was announced the following day. Morally the government was pushed (perhaps not unwillingly), into a corner: long-term funding had to be provided.

Similar considerations have in recent years dictated the relationship between the government and the Building Societies' Association. The mortgage interest rates fixed by the building societies play an important part in the cost-of-living indices by which inflation is measured; and these rates are in turn affected by National Savings interest rates, bank lending rates and, more generally, by the fiscal policy of the Treasury. A decision by the Building Societies' Association to recommend (it cannot insist upon) a raising of mortgage rates will also affect the availability of housing, the level of house prices and even the state of the rented-accommodation market. Until the 1960s the government and the building societies kept each other at arm's length, and were ignorant of each other's problems. The explosion in house prices in the early 1970s brought this splendid isolation to an end. Labour and Conservative governments tried to intervene in the housing market unilaterally. Richard Crossman introduced an option mortgage scheme, to be administered by local authorities, which offered slightly lower mortgage rates than those of the building societies, but with no income-tax relief. Mr Heath's government promoted a 'low-start' mortgage scheme which was equally unspectacular in its results. Early in 1973, in an effort to force the societies to keep down their rates to borrowers, the Conservative government 'invested' £15 millions in the societies, on condition that the mortgage interest rate was held at 9.5 per cent.

By the end of the year the mortgage rate had risen to 11 per cent. But one long-term by-product of this government subvention was the establishment of a Joint Advisory Committee, composed of the chief general managers of the leading building societies (usually past or present members of the Building Societies' Association), officials from the Treasury, the Department of the Environment and the Bank of England, and the Chief Registrar of Friendly Societies, who oversees building society activities. The Joint Advisory Committee enables the societies and the government to exchange ideas on the provision of homes, housing finance and long- and short-term interest rate structures (*The Times*, 15 Apr. 1977:17). But it is also clear that, through the machinery of the Committee, the Treasury and the Building Societies' Association decide jointly on *policy* in the housing sector.

The new relationship between the building societies and the central government goes deeper still. Even if the Treasury holds, as it must, the ultimate trump card, in that, through the statutory powers available to it, it can determine to a large extent the overall structure of national interest rates, nonetheless it is the Building Societies' Association which sometimes carries out that policy. In early 1978, for instance, the government wished to prevent a sudden substantial increase in house prices, and decided that the best way of achieving this was by restricting the amount of money available to potential borrowers for house purchase. It did not raise interest rates, or reduce mortgage tax relief, both of which would have been politically unpopular. Instead it persuaded the Building Societies' Association to restrict funds to those who wished to buy houses (*The Times*, 9 Mar. 1978:1). Because of episodes such as this, there are some who argue that the Association has been 'captured' by the government. Such a conclusion would be altogether too sweeping. The government has taken the Association into a partnership in which there are obligations on both sides: the right of the Association to be consulted, and the central part played by the Association in national housing provision, have been formally recognized.

In the examples cited so far, governments have devolved policy-making, in whole or in part, to pressure groups. But some sanctions have been retained. Motability relies on government goodwill, and is serviced by the Department of Health. The provision of grants to pressure groups can always be halted, particularly if a group is perceived to be acting contrary to declared policy. Where large sums of money are given, as to the building societies, the government, at the same time, buys its way into the decision-making machinery of the recipient groups. But there are instances where governments seem happy to deliver into the hands of a pressure group, or to allow to remain with a group, the entire and unfettered responsibility for an area of public administration, without any reserve powers or financial sanctions. Two very different examples illustrate this trend.

The first concerns the Civic Trust for the North-West, formed in 1961, to which local industries and local authorities subscribe. In the late 1960s the Trust was charged with the task of planning an improvement scheme for the Tame Valley; later this planning role was augmented when the Trust was given responsibility for the site works actually involved in implementing the agreed scheme. The Department of the Environment agreed to deal directly with the Trust, rather than with the multifarious local authorities and public corporations in the area. Its expertise was thus formally recognized and it thereby 'acquired the status and respectability of a statutory body, even though it was a pressure group' (Richardson and Jordan 1979:151).

The second example concerns the administration and policing of the English Sunday trading laws, of ancient vintage but now consolidated in part IV of the 1950 Shops Act. This Act prohibits, with certain specified exemptions, the retail sale of goods on Sundays. However, those who observe the Jewish Sabbath (roughly sunset Friday to sunset Saturday) may apply, to the appropriate local authority, for Sunday trading registration. The Act recognizes that unscrupulous traders may fraudulently misrepresent themselves as observers of the Jewish Sabbath to obtain such registration. In addition, therefore, to imposing penal sanctions (fines and imprisonment) the Act allows the principal religious groups involved, the Jews and the Seventh Day Adventists, to investigate doubtful cases. Section 53 of the 1950 Act, together with regulations, still in force, made under an earlier Act of 1936, allow the Board of Deputies of British Jews and the British Union Conference of Seventh Day Adventists to establish tribunals to which local authorities may refer traders whom they suspect, either of not being adherents of the religion (Jewish or Seventh Day Adventist) they profess, or of having in reality no conscientious objection on religious grounds to trading on the Jewish Sabbath. If such a tribunal finds for the local authority, all Sunday trading registrations held by the miscreant trader are automatically revoked.

These tribunals are run entirely by the respective religious groups, who bear the whole cost of their operation. In relation to the Jews, however, the government has gone much further. A statutory instrument approved by Parliament in 1979 obliges the Board of Deputies of British Jews to establish, at its own cost, a panel, which has the duty of vetting all Sunday trading applications from professing Jews. Without a certificate from this panel no Jewish application for Sunday trading registration can proceed to the appropriate local authority. Although the 'Jewish Tribunal' operates under procedural rules specified by Parliament, the panel can make and amend its own rules as it thinks fit. Tribunal members must be approved by the Home Secretary; panel members require no such approval.

That such a body can be set up seems at first sight extraordinary. But in fact the Labour and Conservative governments which drafted and approved the 1979 regulations had very sound reasons for allowing the panel to be established and to operate in this arbitrary way. Sunday trading is a political minefield. On the Labour side the Union of Shop, Distributive and Allied Workers opposes a change in the law to make Sunday trading generally easier. On the Conservative side the National Chamber of Trade claims that Sunday trading will put up prices. In the background, but still with strong emotional appeal, lurks the Lord's Day Observance Society. During the 1970s there were many attempts by Gentile traders to pass themselves off as Jews or to obtain the services of Jewish 'dummy' directors of firms, or market stall-holders, in order to be able to trade legally on Sundays. The Board of Deputies of British Jews was worried that the image of Anglo-Jewry was suffering thereby. The Home Office was afraid to legislate by means of a public Bill, but when the Board itself suggested that a vetting panel might be established by delegated legislation, initially sceptical civil servants were happy to grasp at a drastic solution, and local authority enforcement officers breathed a sigh of relief. In the interests, therefore, of bureaucratic convenience, political expediency, and cheapness, a substantial section of the Sunday trading laws, affecting the livelihoods of many traders, is now administered by a pressure group, and not by the government at all. This has come about without a word of parliamentary debate or public discussion; the negotiations were carried out secretly between the representative groups involved (such as the Association of Metropolitan Authorities, the National Chamber of Trade and the Market Traders' Association), the Board of Deputies and civil servants in the Home Office (Alderman 1982).

The use of pressure groups in this way also serves to confer legitimacy upon the government action, or inaction, which flows from it. The Board of Deputies has been used by governments since the early nineteenth century to act as an intermediary between Anglo-Jewry and the state. Legislation dating from 1836 gives the President of the Board the sole right to certify orthodox synagogues for the purposes of marriage registration, and the Board has a statutory role in the administration of laws concerning the immigration of aliens. In return for these free services to the state the Board can expect to be regularly consulted by government departments on a very wide range of matters, such as race relations legislation, nationality laws, and the slaughter of food animals.

Administration on behalf of the state, though undoubtedly a burden on a privately-funded body, can thus bring real advantages. The close relationship between the Ministry of Agriculture and the National Farmers' Union has been noted earlier in this chapter. In 1978 the Scottish National Farmers' Union agreed to administer a compensation scheme, to which the British government and the Common Market contributed, to enable payments to be made to farmers in Scotland who had lost livestock in the January 1978 blizzards. Running the scheme in this way allowed the government to deflect criticisms concerning the manner in which the compensation money was distributed: the farmers' own representative body was, after all, responsible (Richardson and Jordan 1979:150). Poultry breeders in Britain are compelled to slaughter not merely birds infected by fowl pest, but also birds which may have come into contact with the infection. In 1981 the government announced that it could not afford to compensate breeders for poultry slaughtered only because of the risk of possible infection, and that it would therefore require the industry to pay the premium on an insurance policy to cover such a risk. A voluntary levy was instituted and paid to a company, British Poultry Health Improvement Schemes Ltd., which effected the insurance. The chairman of the poultry committee of the National Farmers' Union was made one of the directors of this company, and other directors were drawn from various sections of the British Poultry Federation.

The mutual dependence of the government and the National Farmers' Union has often been criticized as too close and unhealthy. If it is true that the Union wields great authority in its dealings with government, it is equally true that the government is able to manipulate the Union for its own ends. Whatever judgement is finally made about this relationship, two basic facts must be recognized. The first is that it is much easier, and therefore less of a burden on the public purse, for the Ministry of Agriculture to deal with one Union than with many farmers individually. The second is that ultimately it is the government – and, since 1973, the Common Market – which decides the level of financial support to the farmers, and that it is the government – and Parliament – which has the final say in matters of agricultural legislation.

Beyond considerations such as these, there are today areas of public administration which *must* be approached via pressure groups:

there is no other way. This was recognized as long ago as 1950, when the Committee on Intermediaries observed (*Report of the Committee on Intermediaries*, Cmnd. 7904, 1950:43–4):

> Trade organizations and similar bodies ... have considerable experience of dealings with Government Departments. It is this experience which especially equips them to perform their intermediary functions – which, however, are usually regarded by the bodies themselves as quite secondary to their main function of advising their own members, and, when consulted by it, the Government, on questions of policy. In the first place, because of that primary function, the organizations have intimate and continuing knowledge of policy. Collectively one of these organizations knows far more of government policy over a wide field than any individual can hope to attain ... Secondly, there exists between these bodies and the Government Departments with which they principally deal close and friendly personal contacts at all levels. The members and officers of the organizations, senior and junior, know their opposite numbers in the departments and have ready access to them. This naturally facilitates the despatch of business. Finally there is continuity on both sides. When a civil servant who has been dealing with his opposite number in an organization on a particular matter moves to other work, his successor will as a matter of course inherit the contact with the organization, and *vice versa* ... In all these activities the organizations rely on the prestige they have acquired both with members and with Departments, and on the confidence which the Departments have in the organizations.

In this way a form of indirect government has developed in Britain: the government relies on pressure groups to administer policy and to police its own members, while the individual members or constituents of the group accept that, though it is naturally always open to them to appeal directly to government, or Parliament, they will normally be expected to make representations through the groups to which they belong; approaching central or local government in this way is also easier, cheaper, and more likely to bring speedy results.

In the arena of public sector wage bargaining the point is too obvious to require detailed elaboration. Civil servants' pay and conditions, for example, must be negotiated through the appropriate unions and associations. In practice it is just not open to individual railwaymen, university teachers or medical practitioners to negotiate their own wage and salary settlements. The railway unions, the Association of University Teachers and the General Medical Services Committee of the British Medical Association thus come to have monopolies of access not only in relation to narrow issues of remuneration, hours of work and so on, but, consequentially, on matters of wider concern to their members; because, once a representative group has achieved an *entrée* to Whitehall, the opening that is created can be used for all manner of purposes, not just that for which the *entrée* was originally intended. And once a group has been accorded full *persona grata* status it can expect to be bedded down snugly within the bureaucratic system. This is what Professor Keith Middlemas has aptly termed 'incorporation': 'the adoption of major interest groups in the governing process' (Middlemas 1979:383); and what Professor Ghita Ionescu has described as 'the politics of concertation', whereby representative governments agree, in the interests of the orderly administration of society, to share the activity of policy-making with corporate forces (Ionescu 1975:1–2). In this situation the function of Parliament is no longer to legislate, but rather to approve 'the legislation hammered out in a complex, largely secret process of consultation and bargaining between the ministers, officials and interest groups concerned; when this happens the government does not govern, in the strict sense, but rather presides over a power-sharing process (Marquand 1980:10–13).

Education is an excellent example of incorporation in practice. The running of the primary and secondary educational system in England and Wales has come to require the active involvement of a host of groups and associations: professional bodies such as the National Union of Teachers and the National Association of Schoolmasters & Union of Women Teachers; the major religious bodies, such as the Church of England and the Roman Catholic Church, which run voluntary-aided denominational schools; the education committees of local authorities, which have their own representative Association of Education Committees; bodies which represent private and independent schools, such as the Headmasters' Conference; a variety of cause groups, such as 'CASE', the Council for the Advancement of State Education, and the Workers' Educational Association; and 'subject area' groups (many composed of teachers and academics), such as the Classical Association, the Historical Association and the Politics Society. While it is not suggested that all of these groups have central roles to play (some of them could no doubt be discarded without affecting the overall structure and functioning of the educational system), the quality of that system depends very much on their active participation in it. In recent years, for example, parent–teacher associations have undertaken the provision of a great deal of school equipment, necessities for many schools rather than luxuries. The National Confederation of Parent–

Teacher Associations not only offers advice on the formation and running of local associations, but will supply a model constitution designed to help avoid conflict with teachers and will also ensure compliance with the Charities Acts, so that the income of a parent–teacher association is not liable to tax. This is a service which no local education authority is capable of providing, and which would otherwise necessitate employing a solicitor or persuading one to give his professional services free.

There is no doubt that the incidence of incorporation has, in respect of certain areas of public administration, increased dramatically over the past thirty years. The relationship between the Ministry of Agriculture and the National Farmers' Union appears to have been used as a model for a new style of indirect government. The 1947 Agriculture Act was followed two years later by the Legal Aid and Advice Act, which established a system of financial aid in respect of civil cases for those without sufficient means to employ lawyers from their own resources. But the Act did not itself say, except in the broadest terms, how the scheme was to be operated; instead, responsibility for running the scheme was and is delegated to the Law Society, which maintains a Legal Aid Committee to decide questions of general policy, together with fourteen Area and thirty-four Local Committees, staffed by solicitors and barristers, to decide upon individual applications for legal aid. A means test is administered, on behalf of the Law Society, by officers of the Department of Health and Social Security, and the cost of the service is met out of a Legal Aid Fund supplied partly from contributions recovered from assisted persons and partly from the Exchequer (Pollock, 1975:46–7). At various times since 1949 the government has, through the Lord Chancellor, used the services of the Law Society to administer other legal aid and advice schemes. In June 1969, for instance, the Labour Lord Chancellor Gardiner authorized the Society to launch a pilot scheme for a salaried solicitor to act, in the London Borough of Camden, as liaison officer between local solicitors and Citizens Advice Bureaux (Jackson 1979:553).

During the 1950s and 1960s, incorporation spread into other fields. At the time of the Suez crisis (1956), and again in 1967, the motoring organizations were involved in government schemes for the rationing of petrol. In 1958 a government Minister described the Royal Society for the Prevention of Accidents as 'the chosen instrument of the Government for road safety services' (HC *Debates*, 21 May 1958: col. 1293). The Society receives government funds to cover salaries and other expenses. Inspectors of the Royal Society for the Prevention of Cruelty to Animals, though without any special legal powers of their own, do in fact act as unpaid government agents to enforce animal welfare legislation. Following the passage of the Wildlife and Countryside Act, in 1981, the government approached the Society to provide (apparently without payment) a certain number of inspectors to exercise surveillance of birds allowed to be kept in captivity under section 7 of the Act. The Society has, for many years, undertaken at its own expense the collection and destruction of stray dogs; successive governments have been happy, and relieved, that it is the Society, and not a government agency, which carries out this task. The Howard League for Penal Reform enjoys a unique relationship with the Home Office on matters of prison policy, and can expect almost as of right to be represented on a wide range of policy-making bodies concerned with the running of the prison system (Cohen and Taylor 1978:3). As we have seen, the voluntary societies that care for the disabled have been given formal roles by statute. Those that care for ex-offenders, such as the National Association for the Care and Resettlement of Offenders, are also heavily involved in the administration of schemes to look after offenders once they are released from prison.

Occasionally, however, a pressure group will be able to achieve by 'private treaty' what the state has not been willing to grant it; that is, it will be able to administer a policy by private arrangements with other groups. Examples of this in relation to the policy processes of central government are rare, for it is doubtful whether such practices would survive for long without a public outcry. Attempts by trade associations to fix prices do occur from time to time, but can generally be brought before the Restrictive Practices Court, established in 1956. In 1981 petrol retailers began to make surcharges for the use of credit-cards by motorists buying petrol. The strict legality of this practice was not in doubt, but other market forces prevailed, there was a slump in petrol prices, and the practice was in many cases abandoned irrespective of the strictures of the Office of Fair Trading. 'Private treaties' are less rare at local level. There are many areas of local concern not covered by statute law, for which no government department is responsible, and which it is beyond the powers of local government officials to control. The result is a system of private law, administered by or on behalf of a pressure group in its own interest and perhaps to the detriment of the interests of others.

In 1981 a new voluntary-aided denominational school was built in a quiet cul-de-sac in a north London suburb. Residents of the cul-de-sac had protested long and loudly when plans for the school were announced, and there was talk of court action to try to reverse the planning decision. The main contention of the local residents was that the cul-de-sac, though large, could not confortably accommodate the motor traffic which it was alleged the school would generate, especially in the mornings. To forestall further protests, the governors of the school came to an agreement with representatives of the residents, to the effect that the governors would instruct parents of children at the school not to park their cars in or drive their cars along the cul-de-sac; any parent disobeying this instruction would, after due warning, have his child or children expelled from the school. The registration numbers of cars parked in the cul-de-sac are noted by school officials, and efforts are made to identify the owners. The governors of the school have, with the approval of the residents, delegated to the headmaster the 'authority' to issue written permissions to certain parents to drive along and park in the cul-de-sac, but only at times and for reasons specified by him. The cul-de-sac is of course a public road; there are no 'yellow lines' or other legally authorized parking restrictions along it length. But the residents have, in this curious and disturbing manner, been able to achieve by private treaty what the state, and the local police, are unwilling or unable to grant them: the exclusion, from the road, of practically all cars belonging to parents of children at the school.

A denominational school in a north London suburb seems a very long way from the *haute politique* of Whitehall. But the privileged position of the residents of that cul-de-sac is in its essentials no different from that of the National Farmers' Union or the Law Society. All these representative groups have been able to have delivered into their hands control over areas of public administration vital to the interests of their members. In this way they have become part of the machinery of the central and local government of the country. If the demands of groups such as these are not met, they have the ability to deploy sanctions. The efficiency of agricultural production demands the co-operation of the farmers. Without the efforts of the Law Society the English legal system would collapse. The effectiveness of Motability, and of the 1981 Education Act, depends on the active continuous involvement of the voluntary societies. If the Anglo-Jewish community were suddenly to withdraw from the administration of the Sunday trading laws, these laws would rapidly fall into disrepute, and the Home Office would be faced at once with a problem of great political sensitivity.

Government thus becomes a prisoner of its own indulgence. What is more, there are some unsavoury instances of what can happen when a pressure group decides to bring its goodwill to an end, or simply not to make it available at all. The attempt by the post-war Labour government to nationalize the iron and steel industry, and the success of the Iron and Steel Federation in frustrating the implementation of the relevant Act, were noted in Chapter 2. In certain respects the Federation was very fortunate. It was obliged to do battle with the government at a time when that government was politically weak; and it could rely on the support of the Conservative Party. It was also lucky in that a general election took place at just the right moment (1950) and with just the right result. In any case, public ownership of the iron and steel industry was not high on Labour's agenda. Had legislation been introduced in 1946 the outcome of the contest between the Labour government and the Federation might have been very different.

So this example is far from typical; but the lesson is very clear. It was learned again, this time by the Conservatives, in the early 1970s, when the Trades Union Congress sabotaged the 1971 Industrial Relations Act. It has been learned many times since, in connection with matters that have not generally been thought of as politically divisive. The administration of local government depends on a partnership between central government and local authorities. There is a need not merely to consult the local authority associations but to obtain their consent where questions of detailed administration are concerned. Whitehall cannot run local government itself and, in any case, running local government through unpaid but elected local councillors is certainly economical and conveniently indirect. The local authority associations are in almost daily contact with government departments, mainly through a network of joint committees: the Housing Consultative Council, the Waste Management Advisory Council, the Consultative Council on Local Government Finance, and many others.

But if this partnership is to work, local government must agree to collaborate. In the summer of 1973 the County Councils Association and the Association of Municipal Corporations, angry at the Conservative government's legislation (then before Parliament) to take responsibility for water services away from elected local authorities into the hands of Regional Water Authorities, advised their members to boycott the work of transferring water-supply and sewerage-disposal functions to the proposed new bodies. The boycott lasted until the following March, a month before the Act was due to come into operation, and was only called off after the Department of the Environment has agreed to allow district councils to retain some sewerage-disposal functions as agents for the new Authorities (Richardson and Jordan 1979:109–13).

It is not necessary, therefore, that a pressure group should possess industrial or financial muscle for it to be able to veto government policies. Indeed, it may not be necessary to use 'muscle' at all. The campaign to introduce child benefit, in 1976–77, was referred to in Chapter 2. The Labour government had originally promised to introduce the benefit, to be paid to wives, but then appeared to hesitate and in 1976 indicated it wished to retain the system of child tax allowances given to husbands. The leak of Cabinet minutes by the Child Poverty Action Group pushed the story into the forefront of public debate. But what appears to have dissuaded the Cabinet from going back on its commitment was a statement of bald fact from the Inland Revenue Staff Federation to the government, that the process of altering, by hand, millions of tax codes had proceeded too far for it to be easily reversed and that, if the government persisted in its reversal of policy, there would be a strike of inland-revenue staff. The victory of pressure groups over the Cabinet was complete.

So far in this chapter we have been considering the relationship between pressure groups and government in the context of policy formation and execution, noting also that the provision of information forms an essential back-cloth to these activities. Pressure groups also perform an essential function of government, and on government's behalf, by monitoring the application of policies already agreed, and by indicating areas where existing policies are felt to be inadequate. Here again, a pressure group will often be in a much better position to survey particular areas of activity than central or local government. A group may well have machinery already in existence, whereas government may have to create such machinery *ab initio*. It may be doubtful whether government machinery would do a better job than the machinery which a group already has set up and in working order. Or a particular monitoring task may be too sensitive or provocative for government to perform; it will be much more politic to leave it to a pressure group to carry out.

Environmental issues provide numerous examples of this monitoring function in action. In 1974 Social Audit, which describes itself as 'an independent non-profit-making body concerned with improving government and corporate responsiveness to the public generally' (Medawar 1979:66), published a report on the government's Alkali Inspectorate. The report – 'a lucid and on the whole accurate piece of investigative journalism' – made some well-substantiated criticisms of the alkali inspectors, whom it condemned for their 'leisurely implementation' of the standards they set, their extreme reluctance to bring offenders (that is, owners of factories emitting more than the legally-permitted levels of pollutants) before the courts, and their 'benign policy of co-operation' with factory-owners (Ashby and Anderson 1981:135). The report, which followed hard upon a number of parliamentary criticisms of the inspectorate, persuaded the Secretary of State for the Environment to order an inquiry into the control of air pollution by the Royal Commission on Environmental Pollution. The Royal Commission, as it happens, vindicated the strategy of the Alkali Inspectorate, but agreed that there had been 'some clumsiness and insensitivity in the Inspectorate's public pronouncements and an air of irritation with those who presume to question the rightness of their decisions' (quoted in Ashby and Anderson 1981:141).

An example with more concrete results is to be found in a study of the origins of the Deposit of Poisonous Waste Act of 1972. At a time when the issue of waste disposal was out of the public eye, and had been placed low down on the agenda for action by the Department of the Environment, the Warwickshire Conservation Society collected evidence of the unauthorized tipping of poisonous wastes, and saw to it that the matter was given extensive media coverage. As a result, legislation which had been envisaged for 1975 was passed, as an emergency, in 1972 (Kimber *et al.* 1974). At local level, indeed, it is more usually a pressure group which will bring to light defects in existing legislation, or point to unsatisfactory environmental situations: a need for traffic lights, or a flyover, perhaps; or the imposition of stricter speed restrictions; or the dangers of atmospheric or river pollution.

Sensitive social issues, such as incest and solvent abuse ('glue sniffing') are much better monitored by pressure groups, for the government has no machinery to do the job itself. Cases of incest are rarely brought to court, and the police have no power to collect evidence of solvent abuse, which is not a criminal offence. In the recent mounting campaign to protect children in care from physical and moral dangers, it has not been the Department of Health which has collected the evidence, but a number of pressure groups such as the National Foster Care Association, the Family Rights Group, the Children's Legal Centre, the National Council for Civil Liberties, and the National Children's Bureau (FitzHerbert 1982). The monitoring of the extent to which local authorities have complied with the requirements of the Chronically Sick and Disabled Persons Act is being carried out through a project established by fifteen major voluntary organizations of and for disabled people, led by the Royal Association for Disability and Rehabilitation. The project investigates the response of local authorities to the Act and reports defaulters to the Minister for the Disabled, or sometimes takes action itself to secure compliance (*The Times*, 26 May 1982:10). Even in areas where the government has or could obtain for itself the power to collect information, it has not always done so. When the Labour government, in 1977–78, wished to keep track of the level of wage settlements, it used information provided by the Confederation of British Industry; the Confederation's monitoring facilities and data bank could not have been improved upon by Whitehall, and it was evident that industry would resent monitoring by its own representative group far less than by a 'socialist' administration.

So pressure groups can find themselves very firmly at the surveillance end of the policy process. Sometimes they will make the first move in establishing this relationship, but sometimes the first move will come from the government. This is particularly true of those government departments and agencies which actually commission research projects. The organization Political and Economic Planning ('PEP') was established in 1931 by a handful of people from the professions, journalism, industry, the civil service and politics, who came together to try to find solutions to Britain's economic and social problems; in 1978 PEP merged with the Centre for Studies in Social Policy to form the Policy Studies Institute. Throughout its existence PEP always enjoyed very close relations with government departments; indeed, in the 1930s a number of senior civil servants helped, anonymously, to write its reports.

In the 1960s PEP was used by government Ministers to trigger action in a number of social fields. In 1966, at the behest of the Race Relations Board, it made a study of racial discrimination, with the purpose of convincing the Cabinet that there *was* an urgent need for further anti-discrimination legislation; its report was published the following year and, according to Home Secretary Roy Jenkins, proved 'decisive' in persuading the Labour administration to pass the 1968 Race Relations Act (Pinder 1981:141–2). In 1969 PEP agreed to undertake a study of the size and rate of growth of the private sector of medical care; the initiative here came from the then Secretary of State for Social Services, Richard Crossman, and the contract was placed by his Ministry. During the 1970s the Manpower Services Commission based a number of its policy decisions on the findings of a PEP survey, which it had sponsored, into the problem of unemployment (Pinder 1981:147; 151).

It is clear from PEP's experience that some pressure groups are in a much more privileged position than others in their relations with government departments. There is a problem of differential access, pre-eminently to Whitehall, which works to the distinct advantage of some groups and to the decided detriment of others. Short of banning all group activity of this sort it is difficult to see how this problem can be overcome. Pressure groups which have something to offer government – information, expertize, administrative services – are bound to find access to government bureaucrats much easier to achieve. Those which have nothing to offer will have to shout long and hard before they are heard; even this may not succeed. Whether it is right to regard such a state of affairs as sinister, or subversive, is a question which will be confronted in the final chapter. Here it must be stated as a fact of political life in modern Britain, and one which has an important consequence: those who would influence government thinking are well-advised to work through an existing, established and accepted group, if they can, than to form a new organization, whose right to be heard and to be consulted may take years to achieve.

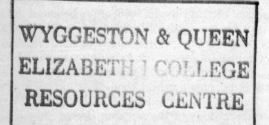

Chapter five
GOING PUBLIC

In previous chapters we have considered the extent and significance of such direct relationships as may exist between pressure groups and the legislative and executive branches of government. Pressure groups which have cultivated and established such relationships are in a position of considerable privilege and, possibly, of some power. These relationships are often highly discreet. Publicity about them is the last thing a pressure group desires; the main concern of the group is to maintain as close a relationship as possible, hidden from the public view, so that negotiations may proceed without fear of public embarrassment.

The need for discretion is also recognized on the government side of the relationship. Tighter state regulation of motor vehicle noise, and proposals for the compulsory wearing of seat belts, have been delayed because the Ministry of Transport did not want to impose them on the motor industry in the face of hostility from the Society of Motor Manufacturers and Traders; in the government's view the preservation of the Ministry's relationship with the Society was more important than a public confrontation (Plowden 1971:383). Although many individual members of the Howard League for Penal Reform favoured the abolition of capital punishment, the League itself was unwilling to organize a public campaign for fear of compromising its relationship with the Home Office. Instead, the National Campaign for the Abolition of Capital Punishment was specially created. The League provided much of the research for the Campaign, and its contacts with government and criminologists proved invaluable. But the League 'was not equipped for or desirous of engaging in large-scale campaigns for abolition, especially since it felt that to do so would jeopardise its standing with the Home Office and prison officials and rebound against its other penal reform activities' (Christoph 1962:186).

It is sometimes argued, therefore, that pressure groups 'go public' from weakness: that a pressure group which launches a public campaign is virtually admitting that its ability to influence Parliament or government discreetly is limited or probably non-existent. But the above examples suggest that this may very often not be the case. The public campaign during 1980 and 1981 in favour of the compulsory wearing of car seat-belts by drivers and front-seat passengers was welcomed by some MPs as a way of breaking the *impasse* created by the Ministry of Transport's deference towards the Motor Manufacturers' Society. The public campaign to abolish the death penalty for murder was the only way such a reform could have been achieved; a private arrangement between the Home Office and the Howard League was (given the extreme political sensitivity of the issue) simply out of the question.

Of course many groups do go public precisely because there is no other way for them to proceed. Their parliamentary leverage may be insignificant. In Whitehall they may be regarded as illegitimate, as *personae non gratae*. They must therefore launch a public campaign, take to the streets, or even flout the law, in order to get their message across. Some writers have tended to belittle the effectiveness and so question the wisdom of public campaigns. Coxall believes that 'on controversial issues, mass publicity may be counter-productive' (Coxall 1981:92). Punnett argues that pressure-group activity through public opinion 'is the most conspicuous but at the same time the least rewarding activity. In the main it is undertaken as a last resort' (Punnett 1976:146). But in the view of the present author those who make such judgements are in danger of missing the purpose of public campaigns, and certainly of ignoring real successes achieved in this way. A public campaign may not have as its objective a dramatic shift in public policy; its object may well be to educate the masses rather than to persuade an elite. Its success may have to be measured in years, perhaps even in decades, rather than in parliamentary sessions.

There are broadly speaking three types of public campaigns available to pressure groups: long-term political campaigns; short-term propaganda, or 'fire-brigade' campaigns; and educational campaigns which, almost by definition, are likely to be long-term rather than short-term. A pressure group may engage in any or all of these, depending on the issues which confront it; and it may aim such a campaign at a mass or at a particular audience. All types of public campaign can achieve positive results.

Educational campaigns comprise much of the activity of cause groups; some cause groups are little more than educational campaigns, and many of them began their lives as such. Since the late nineteenth century there have been a number of organizations whose purpose it has been to educate British public opinion to appreciate the values of free enterprise and freedom from state intervention. Four 'economic' freedom groups have dominated recent activity in this sphere: Aims, formerly Aims of Industry; British United Industrialists; the Economic League; and the Institute of Economic Affairs.

Aims, established in 1942, has from time to time acted on behalf of individual clients. It was responsible for the 'Mr Cube' campaign of the late 1940s which saved the sugar industry (in particular Tate and Lyle) from nationalization. But its general purpose is to promote the virtues of free enterprise, and it does this mainly through the publication of books and pamphlets and by the placing of advertisements in the national press; during general elections its press publicity is particularly colourful and vitriolic. British United Industrialists, formed in 1959 by a merger between the Home Counties Industrialists Association and British Industrialists, is a deliberately clandestine body which apparently sponsors, anonymously, the publication of pamphlets but whose main function seems to be to act as a collecting agency for moneys destined to fill the coffers of the Conservative Party (Nugent 1979:79). The Economic League, established by a consortium of coal and steel owners in 1919, undertakes the mass distribution of leaflets, but also operates 'in company training courses' to which member-companies send their employees, and admits to the production of millions of leaflets and pamphlets designed for distribution within factories, at shop-floor level as well as to management. The Institute of Economic Affairs aims at a very different audience. Set up in 1957 and also financed by industry, it undertakes the scholarly investigation of topics of current interest, and produces booklets written by distinguished specialists; these are advertised for sale in the quality press. The Institute's target audience is thus clearly an elitist one, and comprises those who are likely to participate in the making of decisions at the highest levels.

In December 1975 the 'freedom' lobby acquired a new organization, the National Association for Freedom (NAFF), known from 1979 as The Freedom Association, complete with a fortnightly newspaper, *The Free Nation*. The NAFF is hardly just a propaganda body. Although allegedly non-partisan, its links with the Conservative Party are close; in the late 1970s six Conservative MPs sat on its National Council, and Mrs Margaret Thatcher was the guest of honour at its inaugural subscription dinner in January 1977 (Nugent 1979:88). Other members of its National Council include representatives from big business, and a sprinkling of academics not noted for left-wing views. The NAFF has sometimes indulged in expensive advertising. In October 1978 it placed a large advertisement in *The Times* reprinting an address delivered in Florida by Sir James Goldsmith, headed 'Citizens not Serfs' and asking for donations, because 'the defence of freedom is essential but expensive' (*The Times*, 16 Oct. 1978:5). The main thrust of the NAFF's work, however, has been to educate public opinion through legal action, a topic treated more fully later in this chapter.

In general the publicity undertaken by the freedom associations is not geared to a specific issue, but to general areas of public concern approached with a particular and unashamed bias. Other groups direct their publicity to a specific issue which they wish to bring into public view. Between 1966 and 1969 Parliament legislated on a number of highly controversial social issues, pre-eminently homosexual law reform and abortion law reform (both 1967). In the final stages of these reforms the battleground was mainly a parliamentary one. But each had been preceded by a decade or so of public campaigning, without which it is doubtful whether either reform could have been achieved.

The Homosexual Law Reform Society came into existence as a result of two letters which appeared in *The Times*, on 7 March and 19 April 1958, following publication of the Wolfenden Report on Homosexual Offences and Prostitution the previous September. The letters were signed by forty-eight eminent men and women covering a broad spectrum of political opinion and including two bishops. The Society, by its own admission, 'mostly kept away from Parliament and concentrated upon the Press and the public' (Grey 1975:43). It saw its task as a didactic one. Its secretary, the Rev. A. Hallidie Smith, addressed a large number of meetings of constituency political parties, university societies and local discussion groups. Many members of Parliament, though privately sympathetic to reform, feared a backlash from their constituents; the Society saw its task as the creation of an atmosphere in which the possibility of reform could be aired without hysterical reactions.

In 1960 the first of a series of public meetings was held in London's Caxton Hall. This policy of gradual permeation of 'informed' opinion paid handsome dividends. In July 1964 it became known that the Director of Public Prosecutions had asked all Chief Constables to consult him before prosecuting any man for a homosexual act commited with another consenting adult in private. Press interest in the sympathetic treatment of the phenomenon of homosexuality increased; Fleet Street turned to the Society for background information and articles and women's magazines, in particular, began to discuss the subject frankly and sensitively. The Society's officials were in great demand for speaking engagements. When Mr Leo Abse's private-Member's Bill looked as if it might have failed for lack of time, in the summer of 1967, the Labour government agreed to make extra time available for it; his Bill received the Royal Assent on 27 July. Antony Grey, the Society's secretary from 1962 to 1970, while acknowledging that the series of parliamentary debates between 1965 and 1967 were themselves important in educating public opinion, believes that the Society's chief contribution was 'in creating a climate of opinion in which they [the debates] could be held at all' (Grey 1975:54). Certainly, if the Society had not created this climate of opinion, no-one else would have done so.

An examination of the history of abortion law reform, and of the part played by the Abortion Law Reform Association, reveals a similar pattern. The Association was founded in 1936, mainly as a drawing-room response to alarmingly high maternal mortality rates in Britain at that time, and against a background of widespread and dangerous criminal ('back street') abortions. The Association did what it could, on a very limited budget, to publicise the merits of widening the grounds upon which legal abortions might be performed. But it was never a dynamic or radical body, and the outbreak of war put a sharp brake on its activities. Though it continued in existence it was practically refounded in 1963, following the thalidomide scandal, when the government indicated that abortion on grounds of foetal deformity would not be tolerated. Control of the Association passed to a new generation of reformers, men and women, who were much more alive to the fact that successful parliamentary action must be preceded by massive publicity and propaganda; they were determined to make abortion a subject of public controversy. Newspapers and magazines were deluged with letters and articles; a quarterly newsletter was distributed; and the Association organized opinion polls which demonstrated that the public and the medical profession supported reform. This campaign was not just aimed at the national media. A great deal of emphasis was placed on local action. Groups were formed throughout the country, and the merits of abortion law reform were pressed home in local newspapers and by urging sympathetic constituents to write to their MPs. Early in 1966 the Association began organizing lobbies of Parliament. By the time the Liberal MP, David Steel, introduced his Abortion Bill later that year, nearly 400 MPs had indicated their broad support for reform; Mr Steel's Bill became law in October 1967.

Clearly, a majority of MPs had decided that public opinion had been sufficiently aroused for them to be able to support the Bill and, as with homosexual law reform, the government saw to it that sufficient parliamentary time was made available for its passage. It would be very wrong to conclude that the Abortion Law Reform Association *created* public opinion. It would be right to say that it mobilized public attitudes, strongly aroused after the thalidomide tragedy, and gave them form and direction. As the chroniclers of the Association have written, if the Association 'had not worked steadily for many years on a hostile climate, and campaigned intensively during the last four years [1963–67], reform would not have come as early or as radically as it did' (Hindell and Simms 1974:163).

The campaigns for homosexual and abortion law reform were both educational and political. In neither case was it ever conceivable that success could have been achieved by exclusive concentration on Westminster or on Whitehall; indeed, only in the closing stages of the campaigns did the legislative and executive branches of government become prime targets of the campaigns. But there are instances of public campaigns being aimed almost exclusively at central government or Parliament, or almost exclusively at the general mass audience. Groups concerned to persuade governments to set aside more of the taxpayers' money for overseas aid have an exceedingly difficult time obtaining media coverage of any sort. Although organizations such as Christian Aid, Oxfam and War on Want do engage in mass publicity – advertising, pamphlets, demonstrations and public meetings – such activities are directed mainly towards fund-raising for their own pet projects. The amounts of money collected in this way are, in any case, miniscule compared with government aid overseas. Moreover, there is a strong current of thinking opposed to the giving of charity, and which sees the solutions to problems of world poverty in terms of economic development and a deliberate transfer of resources from the richer countries of the world to the poorer. Groups which think along these lines cannot, for better or worse, hope for widespread public interest; they have to concentrate on meeting individual MPs and on distributing literature to a select audience of Britain's political elite (Fletcher 1968; Young 1975).

Often such supplications will fall on stony ground. Sometimes, however, a group of politicians and civil servants prove sympathetic and responsive. It was well known that in the late 1960s the Ministry of Overseas Development was the source of leaks which gave forewarning of impending cuts in government overseas aid. Contacts between the Ministry and the Voluntary Committee on Overseas Aid and Development were particularly strong, and it seems likely that some of the campaigns waged by the 'aid lobby' at this time were actually inspired by the Ministry at which they were supposedly aimed. The lobby of the House of Commons in July 1969, and the letter-writing exercise which accompanied it, were triggered by a whisper from the Ministry to the effect that a cut in overseas aid was being contemplated; the lobby clearly strengthened the hand of the Minister, Reg Prentice, and the aid programme survived intact. Richard Wood, Conservative Minister for Overseas Development from 1970 to 1974, admitted to the Select Committee on Overseas Aid that he believed it to be right 'to concentrate most available resources [for publicity] on informing those groups and individuals who are in turn conducting extensive publicity and educational campaigns' (quoted in Young 1975:35).

In the case of overseas aid it is indeed difficult to tell where the campaign of the civil servants ends and that of the independent organizations begins (*The Observer*, 12 July 1970:32). By contrast, the bulk of the campaigning by bodies concerned with domestic poverty in Britain is directed at a mass audience. The issues of homelessness and bad housing were taken up by the Notting Hill Housing Trust in the early 1960s; this lead was rapidly followed by a mobilization of Christian groups to fight for better housing provision. In 1966 the British Churches' Housing Trust, the Catholic Housing Aid Society, the National Federation of Housing Societies and the Christian Action 'Homeless in Britain' Fund joined the Notting Hill Trust in creating a national charity, Shelter, under the direction of the journalist Des Wilson. Shelter's aim was to put the issue of slum property on the political agenda, but it also wished to raise money to alleviate the conditions to which it drew attention. It decided on shock tactics, and it went about this task in a professional way, planning every move and employing the services of an advertising agency. In its first six weeks it raised more than £70,000 (D. Wilson, 1967). But this campaign also paid political dividends. The outcry raised by Shelter's frank publicity forced the government – and the opposition – to agree to amend the Housing Subsidy Bill (1967) so as to enable housing associations to acquire funds for buying and improving old properties.

Shelter was both a movement and a pressure group; it sought to influence government, but only as part of a wider campaign in which self-help and self-awareness played an important part. This element was also present in the early years of the Disablement Income Group ('DIG'). DIG originated in a letter about pensions for disabled people which was published in *The Guardian* of 22 March 1965. The writers asked that disabled persons receive a pension as of right to enable them to live in a reasonable degree of independence and dignity in their own homes. The issue had found its time. Run by disabled people whose sincerity and motivation was beyond doubt, DIG became a representative group which no national politician could afford to ignore. Within a few years of its foundation it achieved two remarkable victories: the inclusion of a constant attendance allowance in the National Insurance Act of 1970; and the passage of the Chronically Sick and Disabled Persons Act the same year, making it obligatory upon local authorities to provide services and facilities for disabled people.

How were these victories achieved? Mainly by pitching different publicity campaigns at different levels in society. A demonstration by disabled people in Trafalgar Square (1967) was given saturation coverage in the tabloid as well as in the quality press. Professional social workers were provided with well-researched factual information. A book, entitled *Social Security and Disability*, compared the treatment of disability in Britain with that in the rest of Europe (Frost 1975:87). Programme time was obtained on radio and television. Above all, DIG rapidly achieved a reputation for integrity without loss of partiality. When it approached MPs and Ministers, it was heard with respect but also with awe; its reputation had preceded it.

DIG might have gone about its work in a very different way, by mounting a discreet low-key campaign aimed at Westminster. This might have achieved the same *legislative* result, but would the public at large have been any the wiser about the problems of disability? Almost certainly not. Legislative or administrative action can only go so far in alleviating the worries of the disabled. If public attitudes are to be affected, a parliamentary campaign may be a waste of time. But suppose that a pressure group does not want, primarily, to change the law, but wants instead to change the public perception of a particular issue, or to have laws more rigorously (or, occasionally, less rigorously) enforced? If this is the case, mass campaigning is the only way to achieve the desired result.

In post-war Britain the Campaign for Nuclear Disarmament ('CND') stands out as the most dramatic pressure group to have functioned in this way. Founded the 1957, CND operated at several distinct levels, and was in some respects an umbrella organization under which a variety of campaigns operated at once. It was a movement protesting against all nuclear weapons, at British nuclear weapons, at British membership of the North Atlantic Treaty Organization (strongly influenced by American nuclear policy), and at the defence policy of the Labour Party. In regard to this last aim, the most important mass lobbies CND organized were not at Westminster but at Labour Party conferences. The mass public demonstration was CND's chosen weapon, pre-eminently in the form of the famous Easter marches from the Atomic Weapons Research Establishment at Aldermaston to Trafalgar Square. Some within the movement – The Committee of One Hundred – indulged in non-violent civil disobedience, such as sitting on pavements or in roadways.

CND failed in some of its narrower and more specific aims. Its success at the Labour Party conference at Scarborough, in 1960, when a unilateralist motion was carried, was short-lived, for the policy was reversed the following year. Although Labour fought and won the 1964 general election on a defence policy which renounced independent national control (though not the possession) of nuclear weapons, the Labour government did not halt the building of Britain's Polaris submarine fleet, with its nuclear capability, nor did it withdraw from the North Atlantic Treaty Organization. But CND did, by dint of the personal efforts of every one of its 100,000 or so supporters, succeed in forcing the people of Britain to think seriously about nuclear weapons and the moral and strategic implications of possessing them. Those who supported the nuclear-weapons policy were obliged to defend their views. For the first time since the 1930s Britain's defence policy, and therefore, by implication, its foreign policy, became subjects of domestic concern. In this respect CND was an unqualified success. It had made people think seriously about a subject whereas, but for CND, they might not have thought about it at all.

The history of CND does therefore raise questions about the measurement of 'success' in relation to pressure-group activity, if by success we mean the achievement of specific and tangible aims. For if the aim of a group is to effect long-term changes in the values by which society regulates itself, with the admitted possibility of government action as only one of a number of options open to it, then very public campaigning must be its chosen weapon. In recent decades a number of groups have been formed with such ends in view; many of these groups are rooted in Christian beliefs. The National

Festival of Light held mass rallies in Trafalgar Square in 1971 and 1972 to draw attention to the 'moral pollution' which its supporters felt had taken place in England; a quarterly broadsheet is distributed through a variety of sympathetic organizations (Capon 1972:86). The Responsibile Society, formed in 1971, has a more secular approach, claiming that its primary aim 'is the encouragement of responsible behaviour in sexual relationships by educating and informing the public about the real consequences of irresponsibility' (quoted in Cliff 1979:129). Its membership is numbered in hundreds rather than in thousands, and it sees its role as an educative one, sponsoring research and disseminating the results within the intelligentsia.

The National Viewers' and Listeners' Association ('NVALA') is by far the most significant of these groups. It grew out of the Clean-Up TV Campaign ('CUTV'), founded in 1964 by two Midlands housewives, Mary Whitehouse and Norah Buckland, who shared a deep concern that the sexual upbringing of schoolchildren was being undermined by television programmes which bred a 'sub-Christian' concept of life. A meeting called at Birmingham Town Hall on 5 May 1964 was rapturously attended and brought instant nationwide publicity. It was clear that the aims of CUTV had wide support in the community; the BBC, in particular, was forced to sit up and take notice. At the same time it was evident that the politicians, industrialists, church leaders and housewives who supported CUTV shared other concerns. Mrs Whitehouse explained that CUTV 'very quickly moved from being a grass roots protest against gratuitous sex and violence and bad language to being a group which was producing philosophy, tactical activities for structural change' (quoted in Tracey and Morrison 1979:47). An organization with broader aims was clearly required. On 16 March 1965 NVALA was launched.

The impact of NVALA has been obscured by that of Mrs Whitehouse, its leading light. It was Mrs Whitehouse who in 1974 brought a private prosecution under the 1824 Vagrancy Act against a London cinema for allegedly allowing indecency in a public place by showing a certain Franco-Italian film (*Observer*, 7 Apr. 1974:5). Two years later it was Mrs Whitehouse who persuaded the Home Secretary to refuse entry into Britain to the Danish director Jens Jorgen Thorsen, who wished to make a film about the sexual life of Jesus of Nazareth. It has also been alleged that Mrs Whitehouse kept the American film *Deep Throat* out of England by tipping off customs officials that it was about to be brought into the country (Wootton 1978:40). And it was certainly Mrs Whitehouse who brought about the successful prosecution of *Gay News* (1977) for publishing what was held to be a blasphemous libel, a poem about the Crucifixion.

The role of NVALA has been rather different. Although a highly articulate group, it cannot claim to be representative of the community. Research suggests that its support is mainly middle-class, female and elderly, that it is over-represented by those in rural areas, the clergy, the older-established professions, small businessmen, traders and shopkeepers (*Sunday Times*, 12 Feb. 1978:17). It is not automatically consulted by government departments, with which its relations are often very tense, and it is certainly not a necessary or essential component of any area of public administration. But its ability to mobilize an important section of public opinion is a formidable weapon. It does not waste time trying to convert those whom it knows are likely to be hostile to its views. It concentrates on the Conservative Party, the churches, the religious press and provincial newspapers, which are likely to be less liberal in outlook than Fleet Street and which welcome contributions from controversial national personalities to relieve the monotony of local tittle-tattle.

Its defence of religious values and its opposition to secularist and permissive trends on radio and television may at first sight seem Canute-like or ostrich-inspired. But in going public (for there is nowhere else to go in these matters) NVALA certainly touches sensitive areas of national consciousness. It is quite obviously treated with a healthy respect by the BBC, the Independent Broadcasting Authority and by the British Board of Film Censors. Yet its very success in fostering moral outrage has disadvantages. Mrs Whitehouse herself evokes deep respect among her followers but also deep anger among those who disagree with her. NVALA is a wonderful machine for public propaganda, but it is less useful as a parliamentary lobby. The campaign against child pornography, which resulted in the passage of the 1978 Child Protection Act, was not undertaken by NVALA but by a 'front organization', ABUSE; only after the campaign had commenced was NVALA 'brought into the fray as a spontaneous ally' (McCarthy and Moodie 1981:51).

It should not be thought, however, that it is only the great 'public morality' campaigns which seek to change values in society. There are many other examples. In 1981 a consortium of Britain's leading manufacturers and metal processors launched a national campaign to promote the collection and recycling of empty tins, setting up collection points in twenty towns and cities similar to the 'bottle banks' initiated by glass manufacturers some years previously. The consortium promised a payment to charity of £5 for every ton of metal collected (*The Times*, 9 Oct. 1981:4). 'Planning Aid', a body of professional planners who give free help to people unable to afford expert advice, if they wish to make or to challenge planning applications, also has the wider aim of pinpointing weaknesses and loopholes in the British planning system, both locally and nationally (Drinkwater 1982). In November 1981 Action on Smoking and Health, in conjunction with the Health Education Council, sent leaflets to Britain's 25,000 family doctors urging them to 'prescribe' the giving up of smoking by their patients. This was part of an educational campaign against smoking, but it should also be seen within the context of a wider effort to persuade the government to take a tougher stand against the advertisement and sale of tobacco products (*The Times*, 20 Nov. 1981:4).

The nature of a particular pressure group, the sort of impact it seeks and the ends it has in view, may therefore dictate that a public campaign is essential, even if the campaign is political rather than educational. Indeed, even in those instances where a campaign *is* essentially political, often it will do no harm for a public relations exercise to hover in the background, less as a means of persuading governments than as an indication of serious intent. In July 1981 the music industry learned that the government had ruled out the possibility of a levy on blank tape-recorder cassettes. The British Phonographic Industry Ltd., the Musicians Union and the Music Publishers' Association had argued that allegedly illegal home-taping of records and radio music on domestic cassette recorders was depriving record companies and artists of royalties and was costing the music industry millions of pounds each year. But whereas a loss of £200 millions was claimed for 1977, the Department of Trade put the figure at only £50 millions. When the government decision was announced, the music and record industries placed a series of half-page advertisements in *The Times* and *The Guardian* claiming that 'Home taping is wiping out music' and carrying the signatures of dozens of recording artists representing every shade of musical taste. The campaign itself became a news item. The government's mind was, to be sure, not immediately changed. But by July 1982 it was clear that the Department of Trade was having second thoughts (*The Times* 28 Oct. 1981:7; 20 July 1982:2).

It is at the 'fire-brigade' level that public campaigning becomes indispensable. As budget-day approaches it is certain that a number of pressure groups, anxious to catch the attention of the Chancellor of the Exchequer, but afraid that they might not, will appeal to the masses. In January 1982 the National Federation of Retail Newsagents and the Retail Confectioners' and Tobacconists' Association, supported, it would appear, by the Tobacco Advisory Council, launched a two-pronged pre-emptive strike against the possibility of an increase in tobacco duty in the forthcoming budget. A series of newspaper advertisements claimed that the tax on cigarettes proportionate to their cost was greater than the tax levied on betting, the cinema, petrol or 'dining out', and the advertisements invited readers to sign copies of a national petition, addressed to the Chancellor, in their local tobacconist or newsagent (*Sunday Times*, 24 Jan. 1982:6). The petition attracted well over a million signatures; the budget increase in tobacco duty was less than expected. It is just possible, given the undoubted unpopularity of the government at that time, that the two were connected.

At local level fire-brigade campaigns are exceedingly common. Surprisingly, most people take little continuous interest in what goes on in their immediate neighbourhood. Organizations must be hastily formed or re-formed to deal with situations as they arise. The campaign to prevent Cublington (Wing) from becoming London's third airport has already been mentioned. The columns of any local newspaper will provide many more examples. In 1974 a movement entitled 'Surrey and Kent Against the Rail Link' was launched to prevent high-speed trains being routed through the Marden Valley towards the projected Channel Tunnel. Two years later a 'Save Our Seafront Action Committee' was formed at Dover to protest against a proposed new Hoverport (Wootton 1978:175).

To be effective fire-brigade campaigns need almost instant leverage. How is this obtained? If a general election is close at hand the weapon is ready-made, though its impact will of course depend upon election outcomes. In the late 1940s, and again prior to the general elections of 1959 and 1964, campaigns were mounted against the proposed nationalization of the iron and steel industry. We have seen that the campaign of the late 1940s was successful (see Chapter 2). In 1959 Labour lost the election, and in 1964 its majority, six, was too small to make re-nationalization practicable. But in 1966 Labour was returned with a much bigger majority, and no amount of protestations could save the iron and steel industry from the fate of public ownership once again.

A more successful campaign was that launched by the sugar corporations during the general elections of 1950 and 1951, in which the cartoon figure of 'Mr Cube' played a central part. The campaign was entrusted to a steering committee of Aims of Industry and Tate and Lyle, and was allotted a budget estimated at £250,000. Since practically every household in the country bought sugar it was only prudent to ensure that Mr Cube, defending free enterprise, appeared on sugar packets. Free models of Mr Cube were given away to schoolchildren. A 'Sugar Consumers' Petition' was advertised in the press. The nation's foremost radio and television reporter, Richard Dimbleby, recorded interviews with Tate and Lyle staff; 4 million copies of the record were distributed (Finer 1966:94–5). Not only was sugar saved from nationalization then; Labour has never subsequently dared to resurrect the proposal.

If a fire-brigade campaign has no general election to help it along, it has only three alternatives: either it must appeal to the self-interest of those in authority; or it must appeal to their better judgment; or it must confront them with a situation potentially far more damaging than that envisaged by the policy they wish to pursue. The first two alternatives are fraught with hazards. To appeal to the self-interest of Members of Parliament requires discretion and tact, but it can yield useful results. The campaign by light-socket manufacturers (see Ch. 3), undertaken at very short notice, was nevertheless perfectly executed, partly because it singled out for special attention those MPs with light-socket factories in their constituencies. To appeal to the better judgment of MPs and civil servants is likewise hazardous. But if a case is presented cogently and reasonably it may be accepted. In early 1982 the government and the House of Commons accepted the view of the Take Away & Fast Food Federation, in relation to legislation then before Parliament, that take-away food shops such as Macdonald's, Wimpy and Kentucky Fried Chicken should be allowed to remain open between 11.00 p.m. and midnight, because a great deal of business was done between those hours and unemployment might result if an earlier closing time was enforced.

Confrontation is not a tactic many pressure groups employ. It is often an act of desperation and it may involve activities of dubious legality. But it is most definitely not a sign of weakness, and it can achieve a remarkable degree of success either in a fire-brigade situation or as part of a long-term campaign.

The *modus operandi* of the 'Stop The Seventy Tour Campaign' ('STST') illustrates the advantages of confrontation to achieve a short-term objective. The campaign grew out of opposition in Britain to the domestic policies of the South African government and, in particular, out of a desire to break sporting links with South African teams as a means of pressurising the South African government to alter those domestic policies. Since no British government was willing, formally, to prevent the entry into the United Kingdom of

South African sportsmen, the campaign also had as its purpose a demonstration, to British sporting authorities and to the British government, that all manner of unspeakable (or at least unspoken) consequences would ensue if South African teams were invited to and allowed to enter Great Britain.

STST was triggered by the announcement that a South African cricket tour of England was to take place in the summer of 1970. Peter Hain, a native of South Africa and then a member of the British Young Liberal Movement, was instrumental in persuading the Young Liberals to pledge themselves in January 1969 'to take direct action to prevent scheduled matches from taking place unless the 1970 tour is cancelled' (Hain 1971:115). What this 'direct action' might be was never spelled out, but in the months which followed the phrase was to crop up again and again and others, equally sinister, were added: 'direct action tactics'; 'civil disobedience'; 'direct-action demonstrations'. A private South African cricket tour in the summer of 1969 was physically disrupted, as was a Davis Cup tennis match between South Africa and Britain played at Bristol in July.

When STST was officially launched, in September 1969, these 'token disruptions' were used to bring home the point. 'Next summer', Peter Hain wrote to *The Guardian*, 'could see a season consisting of an endless series of protests and disruptions.' (Hain 1971:121) A tour of England and Wales by the South African Springboks rugby football team turned into a series of ugly pitched battles and gave rise to a debate in the House of Commons. The reaction of the police and the rugby officials played into the hands of the protesters; in using force to remove protesters from playing areas the police appeared to be taking sides in the dispute, and the brutality of some civilian 'stewards' could not be denied. Chief Constables became nervous. The Home Office agreed to meet a delegation from STST to discuss police behaviour. After the rugby tour discreet pressure was brought to bear by the Home Office upon the Cricket Council, so that the original schedule of twenty-eight matches was cut to twelve. Meanwhile, in the early months of 1970 political support for the motives, if not the methods, of STST grew, particularly within the trade union movement and the British Council of Churches. Intermittently, too, pressure was brought to bear upon the British government from Commonwealth countries. Buckingham Palace announced that the Queen would not be making her traditional visit to the Lord's Test Match. On 21 May 1970 the Home Secretary, James Callaghan, appealed to the Cricket Council to call off the South African tour 'on grounds of broad public policy'. The following day the tour was cancelled.

The morality of STST's methods have been the subject of much debate. Of their efficacy there can be no doubt. STST was not a well-drilled or well-financed organization. Indeed, it was not a formal organization at all; its headquarters appear to have been a Fleet Street public house, it hired no public relations consultants, and all its members were unpaid volunteers. But it learned very early on the all-important lesson that (at least up to a point) all publicity is good publicity, that 'direct action' tactics are much more sophisticated than stereotyped conventional demonstrations (Hain 1971:148).

But it would be erroneous to suppose that direct action must involve violence. The campaign to legalise Citizens' Band (CB) radio shows how direct action of the most peaceful kind can also be successful. CB radio originated in the United States in the 1960s as a result of the public sale of ex-army radio equipment; installed in cars and lorries, CB transceivers enable drivers to keep in contact with each other, perhaps to warn of road hazards, perhaps to call for help following an accident, perhaps to alert others to the presence of police speed-traps. The *use* (but not possession) of such equipment was illegal in Britain. But professional smugglers managed to import thousands of sets and found a seller's market awaiting them. Initially transactions were conducted via the Isle of Man, where the sale of CB transceivers was never contrary to the law. Later sales were made quite openly on the British mainland. Use of CB sets developed into an epidemic which neither the police nor the courts could control. In 1980 there were 457 convictions for using illegal equipment or for using CB sets without a licence; only one person who refused to pay a fine was imprisoned (*The Times*, 3 Nov. 1981:4). At the same time, the Home Office claimed to be receiving about 1,000 letters every week complaining that illegal CB-users were interfering with television and radio reception and with police and ambulance wavelengths.

Sensing defeat, the government prepared a compromise. The Home Office announced that it was willing to legalize the use of CB radio, not on the powerful AM (amplitude modulation) frequency on which the illegal sets operated, but on the more localized FM (frequency modulation) waveband. And the government negotiated, not with the illegal CB-users, but with the officials of the National Committee for Legalization of Citizens' Band Radio, whose chairman, Mr Ian Leslie, was largely instrumental in drafting the code of conduct issued by the Home Office when CB radio, on the FM frequency, was legalized in November 1981. Illegal users have therefore had to have their transceivers modified in order to comply with the law; but the principle of CB radio use has been conceded.

In the case of CB radio it might be argued that those who used illegal methods did not win a complete victory. Indeed, many illegal users were not consciously trying to exert pressure on the government at all, though that is what their activities amounted to. Nor is there any suggestion of collusion between the illegal users of CB radio and the legitimate National Committee. Nevertheless, successful illegal use was the single most important factor leading to the legalization of this form of communication.

There is a lesson here, unpalatable to some, no doubt, but unmistakeable. As a form of public pressure, illegality can pay handsome dividends. Sometimes the illegality can be quite open and deliberate. In November 1976 the Sikh community was successful in obtaining statutory exemption from the law requiring motorcyclists to wear crash helmets. The Sikh religion prohibits the wearing of a head-covering other than the turban, and Sikh motorcyclists had demonstrated their willingness to face criminal charges rather than forsake the precepts of their faith. Parliament gave way to them. Their success has led to a wider campaign, the Motor Cycle Action Group, which calls for all motorcyclists to be allowed to ride their machines bare-headed if they wish; the Group organizes rallies of bare-headed motorcyclists to prove its point (*The Times*, 7 Dec. 1981:3).

Acts of doubtful legality may also be used to bring public attention to bear on particular problems or issues. Members of the conservationist pressure group 'Greenpeace' have chained themselves to the gates of the Norwegian Embassy in London in protest against inhumane harpoon methods allegedly used by Norwegian whalers; they left after an inquiry had been promised, so their protest must have made some impression (*The Times*, 20 Nov. 1981:3). Another conservation group, 'Sea Shepherd', sprays seals pups with a blue dye to render their pelts worthless; this saves the pups from being shot or bludgeoned to death for their skins. The pups are obviously grateful; in addition, the action has led to the arrest of Sea Shepherd members and, as a consequence, to more publicity for the group's work (*The Times*, 5 Nov. 1981:6). Members of the Animal Liberation Front have found themselves in court, and occasionally in gaol, for liberating animals they claim are held in unfit conditions or are destined for laboratory experiments. The Hunt Saboteurs Association practically invites penal sanctions as its members go about their duties, which consist not merely in sabotaging hounds but also in liberating animals supposedly destined for experiments. Given a suspended prison sentence for his part in an 'early morning raid' to liberate some beagles, the Association's secretary was reported as having declared 'The law on vivisection has not been changed for more than a hundred years and we shall continue with our activities until it is' (*The Times*, 5 Mar. 1982:3).

In all these cases important educational or public relations goals have been attained by methods which have relegated the law of the land to a position of secondary importance. Most public relations exercises by pressure groups are far less traumatic, though they certainly do not lack ingenuity. The National Anti-Vivisection Society has used newspaper advertisements in an effort to raise money to campaign against the fatal LD50 test widely used on animals to investigate the toxicity of cosmetics, pesticides, drugs, food additives, weedkillers and detergents (*The Times*, 9 Mar. 1982:1). A newspaper advertisement placed in November 1981 by the Society for the Protection of Unborn Children, and attacking the so-called 'mercy killing' of severely deformed babies, consisted largely of a message written, with her foot, by Marilyn Carr, herself born severely handicapped, who had stood as 'Independent Pro-Life Candidate' at the Croydon North-West by-election the previous month (*The Times*, 23 Nov. 1981:4). During the lifetime of the Labour government of 1974–79 insurance companies included anti-nationalization leaflets with the bonus notices issued to their policy-holders. More recently the Association of Metropolitan Authorities has spent large sums on advertisements ('Keep It Local') criticising Conservative government proposals to curb the power of local authorities to levy rates. In March 1982 the Police Federation, as part of its campaign to convince MPs of the need to restore the death penalty for the murder of police officers, included in its newspaper-advertisement campaign a form, returnable to the Federation, urging the restoration of capital punishment for murder; many thousands of these forms were returned, enabling the Federation to claim that 'public opinion' supported its views (*The Times*, 17 Mar. 1982:5).

At about the same time the Nuclear Power Information Group, sponsored by a consortium which included British Nuclear Fuels, the Central Electricity Generating Board and the United Kingdom Atomic Energy Authority, indulged in a newspaper campaign to reassure the public about the safety aspects of nuclear energy; readers of its advertisements were invited to write for a free copy of 'The Facts About Nuclear Energy' (*Sunday Times*, 14 Mar. 1982:4). And the Greater London Council, forbidden by the Court of Appeal from pursuing its 'Fares Fair' policy for London Transport, spent a great deal of ratepayers' money on an advertising campaign which invited ratepayers to send to their MPs a coupon calling on the government 'to take immediate action to enable the GLC to maintain its present low fares policy without any reduction in services' (*Hendon Times*, 4 Mar. 1982:2).

Do such campaigns have any impact? The answer to this question depends upon the view one takes of their purpose. The fact that the stated objective of a publicity campaign is achieved does not necessarily mean that the achievement was due to the campaign. One of the objects of a campaign may be merely to keep a particular issue before the public eye; advertisements certainly do this, though the cost in money terms is high. Letter-writing exercises are much cheaper, but there are pitfalls in this type of pressure. MPs and local councillors are quite used to receiving large amounts of correspondence. When much of this correspondence concerns one particular issue, legislators and civil servants cannot plead ignorance of the subject-matter. But orchestrated campaigns of this sort can easily backfire. A duplicated letter signed many times over (or, worse still, a letter copied out word for word, grammatical errors and all) is bound to have less impact than a smaller number of individually-written pieces of correspondence, each, perhaps, addressing the same issue but from a slightly different angle. When MPs and government departments receive stereotyped or identical letters they duplicate and return identical replies. An individually-written letter must have its own tailor-made reply; on this score alone it achieves an impact.

Any form of public campaigning depends crucially on the reaction of the media. The mere fact that a campaign is being launched may not in itself be newsworthy. Newspapers, radio and television need and demand a positive element of attraction to induce them to 'cover' a campaign. A favourite device used by modern British pressure groups is the issuing of a 'report' or a 'survey'. A campaign in 1982 by the National Consumer Council against unnecessary bureaucratic delays was prefaced by the publication of a survey purporting to show that a high proportion of 2,000 consumers interviewed regarded local and national government departments as officious, incompetent and inflexible (*The Times*, 31 Dec. 1981:2). A dossier, entitled *Britain's Battered School Children*, issued in January 1982 by the Society of Teachers Opposed to Physical Punishment, and cataloguing 158 attacks by teachers on pupils, achieved wide media coverage within the context of a public debate then under way on the question of corporal punishment in schools (*Sunday Times*, 24

Jan. 1982:4). The Right to Fuel Campaign, in urging the restoration of electricity supplies to an estimated 30,000 households during the savage winter of 1981–82, sponsored an 'independent review' of the code of practice followed by the electricity boards and claimed that since most of the people disconnected simply could not afford to pay their fuel bills, all disconnections should be suspended (*The Times*, 14 Jan. 1982:2).

A second device much favoured nowadays is legal action. Obviously not every pressure group is in a position to take cases to court, or can afford to do so. In a great many instances legal action would, in any case, be entirely inappropriate. But there are circumstances in which legal action can be useful not only in itself but as part of a wider campaign of pressure. In 1976 the National Association for Freedom gave financial assistance to the Tameside Parents Education Group in their contention (upheld by the House of Lords) that Tameside District Council had no right to introduce comprehensive education. The National Association also gave legal support to the management of Grunwick Film Processing Laboratories in their epic successful struggle against conceding trade-union negotiating rights. In January 1977 the National Association obtained an injunction in the Court of Appeal against the postal workers' boycott of mail and telecommunications to South Africa, though the Lords subsequently reversed this decision. More recently the National Association has successfully taken to the European Court of Human Rights at Strasbourg the cases of three British Rail staff who were dismissed for not joining a trade union. This attack on the closed shop generated a great deal of public sympathy for workers refused employment in this way, and undoubtedly helped create a climate of opinion favourable to the legislative attack on the closed shop carried out by the Conservative government in 1981–82.

Legal action on this scale will always attract media coverage. A report or survey may also do so, though more easily in the press – and the quality press at that – than on television. Television coverage of the activities of a pressure group is highly circumscribed. If the campaign is at all intellectual, coverage is likely to be restricted to a late news magazine programme, such as 'Newsnight' on BBC2. In any case television coverage is, not unnaturally, geared to what is visually effective. And that is why 'demonstrations' have been so popular with pressure groups in the post-war period. A mass demonstration, particularly outside the Palace of Westminster, has a very good chance of attracting the television cameras. For a great many groups, therefore, 'lobbying' of MPs does not primarily mean seeing MPs at the House of Commons and seeking to persuade them of the rectitude of a particular viewpoint. It means, quite simply, holding a mass demonstration *outside* the Houses of Parliament and obtaining maximum media coverage thereby.

The mass lobby of Parliament is thus not a lobby at all, if by lobby (to revert to the definition given at the beginning of Ch. 1) we mean the attempt directly to influence MPs or to solicit their votes. In the modern mass lobby, numbers count almost as much as arguments. When tens of thousands of people converge on Westminster only a few hundred gain admittance to the Central Lobby of Parliament. There, only constituents with advance appointments can be reasonably sure of seeing their MPs; and, if they do, the interview is likely to take place in a cramped corner of the lobby or in some alcove where the noise of other lobbyists is hopefully not too distracting. The Serjeant-at-Arms has been authorized to refuse MPs all accommodation to interview lobbyists other than in the Grand Committee Room in Westminster Hall. But this room will almost certainly already be in use for MPs to address other lobbyists not lucky enough to gain admittance to the Central Lobby; a few constituents may be able to ask questions, but in general the proceedings in the Grand Committee Room consist of the converted preaching to the converted. The police make certain that no lobbyist can proceed from the Grand Committee Room to the Central Lobby without queuing again on the pavement (or sometimes in the road) outside. Many constituents, even those with specific written appointments to see their MPs, are never allowed into Parliament at all, for the press of people simply cannot be accommodated within the precincts of the Palace of Westminster.

The irony of this state of affairs will not be lost on those who know how lobbying originated, and what its purpose was. In the words of the Labour MP Arthur Latham, Parliament 'has learnt to cope with the mass lobby to such an extent as to make it ineffective, apart from the valuable broad propaganda effect which a demonstration may achieve' (A. Latham 1978). Interviews in the Central Lobby are not televised. But nurses or miners congregating for many hours, in large numbers, in St Margaret Street, Westminster, are almost certain to attract media coverage. And, in all probability, that (and not a meeting with a Member of Parliament) will have been the real purpose of the 'lobby'. Going public may of course be a last-ditch effort to attract the attention of those in authority. But it is not usually so, nor is it really a sign of weakness. It is often an important component of a wider campaign, and it may be an essential pressure-group activity. It can be as effective as discreet negotiations, and it can bring valuable rewards.

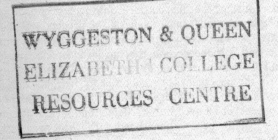

Chapter six
THE GOVERNING PROCESS

Probably no facet of modern British government has generated more suspicion, mistrust and even fear than the activities of pressure groups. To constitutional purists they still appear as an intrusion, often unwarranted, into the democratic process, an extra 'estate' which is, moreover, beyond public accountability or control. Electors choose Members of Parliament who legislate on their behalf and who are answerable to them for their actions. The MPs, in turn, sustain a government; but that government, too, is answerable, to Parliament, for its policies. In what the late Professor John Mackintosh (a parliamentarian as well as an academic) aptly termed 'the Westminster Model', pressure groups have, apparently, no place; in his standard work on British government Professor Mackintosh reminds us that it is still thought to be 'unconstitutional' to allow a pressure group to see the draft of a clause in a Bill, because convention demands that Parliament must be the first to see the actual wording of a legislative proposal; all that a pressure group may be told in advance is the content of the clause (Mackintosh 1982:29).

Of course the vital part nowadays played by pressure groups in the process of government is widely recognized. If parliamentary democracy means anything more than the act of voting once every five years or so, then it demands the active and continuous participation of citizens in government; often (as with agricultural policy, for example) this participation is essential to the efficient functioning of government. We might also note that, in proportion as political parties and MPs have fallen in public esteem in Britain since the Second World War, so resort to pressure groups has steadily increased. The number of non-voters at British general elections has grown from an average of 20.2 per cent of the electorate in the five general elections between 1950 and 1964 to an average of 25.6 per cent in the five general elections since 1966. The results of a number of surveys have shown that among ordinary voters there is a widespread feeling of political impotence and a low opinion of the electoral process, of politicians and of Parliament (Finer 1980:130–1). A Gallup survey for BBC Television a week before the 1979 general election revealed that 21 per cent of respondents felt their opinion of politicians had gone down as a result of the election campaign; a Gallup survey the following October showed that though confidence in the honesty of doctors and police officers remained high, so far as MPs were concerned it was low (*British Public Opinion*, i, 1980:25).

People who wish to change Parliament's mind, to influence government thinking or simply to bring about the public airing of a grievance or a point of view, do not join a political party. Neither do they wait until a general election forces their MPs to pay attention to what they have to say. They form or join pressure groups. In consequence, a great deal of the time of government and Parliament is occupied with the consideration of the views these groups put forward. Not only are there more pressure groups active in British government now than there have ever been; these groups appear to wield more power than previously and (some would argue) more power than is perhaps healthy in a democracy like ours.

Here are some of the stories, concerning pressure groups, reported in *The Times* during the period October 1981 to January 1982. On 21 October 1981 *The Times* reported a speech by Dr John Havard, secretary of the British Medical Association, who claimed that the law allowed 'fanatical and moralistic' pressure groups to hound doctors in the courts. Some days later, during the trial at Leicester Crown Court of Dr Leonard Arthur (accused and subsequently acquitted of attempting to murder a baby), Sir Douglas Black, President of the Royal College of Physicians, declared from the witness box that organizations such as 'LIFE' and 'EXIT' were 'helping to destroy the confidence of doctors and nurses' (*The Times*, 31 Oct. 1981:2). EXIT is an organization set up to promote the idea of voluntary euthanasia. LIFE, organized originally to fight the 1967 Abortion Act, has more recently campaigned on the issue of 'mercy killings'; according to *The Times* (6 Nov. 1981:2) it was the chairman of LIFE who had reported Dr Arthur to the police.

But, having recorded the British Medical Association as *objecting* to the activities of pressure groups, *The Times* carried a report (11 Dec. 1981:2) that the Association was itself refusing to co-operate with an inquiry by the Department of Health into the cost and efficiency of family practitioner services. A few days later the Motor Agents' Association advised its petrol-retailer members to ignore a government ruling that the practice of surcharging customers who bought petrol by means of credit cards should end. And early in the new year *The Times* (14 Jan. 1982:3) reported that after two months of bargaining the Society of London Art Dealers had condescended to agree to make available to the Office of Fair Trading the body of its evidence on the so-called 'buyer's premium' charged by auctioneers; the Office was thus enabled to proceed with an investigation into whether the auction houses of Sotheby's and Christie's had colluded over the introduction of the premium, in 1975, and whether these firms were therefore in breach of fair trading practices.

The above examples have not been selected at random. They have been chosen in order to demonstrate, *inter alia*, (1) that modern British pressure groups can be very powerful; (2) that public policy is often dictated or strongly influenced by the interaction of different and competing groups; (3) that good government demands the co-operation of pressure groups. It is not only the 'big battalions' of industry, such as the Iron and Steel Federation in 1950–51 and the trade union movement in 1969 and 1971, which are able to exercise a veto over the intentions of government and Parliament. In December 1976 the United Road Transport Union announced that drivers delivering bread would boycott shops and supermarkets which tried to make large cuts in bread prices the following year; this action had the approval of many bakers, and effectively frustrated the efforts of the Labour government to encourage lower prices for basic bread products (*The Times*, 23 Dec. 1976:2). The policies pursued by the British Medical Association in relation to family practitioner efficiency studies, or by Sikh motorcyclists in relation to the compulsory wearing of crash helmets (see Ch. 5), are thus in a long tradition of pressure-group response to unwelcome activity by the legislative and executive organs of government.

At the same time these examples emphasize that the approval of the relevant pressure groups is an essential component of the process by which the actions of government are legitimized. Not only is such approval essential in itself; the leading spokesmen of pressure groups must be drawn into the governing process. The representatives of the groups are invited to serve on a wide range of government inquiries and advisory bodies. Richardson and Jordan point out that W. C. Anderson, general secretary of the National and Local Government Officers Association from 1957 to 1973, served on the Fulton Committee on the Civil Service (1966–68); the National Insurance Advisory Committee (1970–76); the Industrial Injuries

Advisory Council (1970–74); and the Royal Commission on Civil Liability and Compensation for Civil Injury (1973). Sir Michael Clapham, a past president of the Confederation of British Industry, was a member of the Industrial Reorganization Corporation (1968–71); the Standing Advisory Committee on Pay of the Higher Civil Service (1968–71); and the Review Body of Doctors' and Dentists' Remuneration (1968–70) (Richardson and Jordan 1979:69–70).

In short, the influence of pressure groups is to be found at all levels in the organs and decision-making machinery of British government. This is inevitable. But whether the influence is for good or for ill is a matter of great dispute. The important line of demarcation in government between the making of decisions and the influencing of the making of decisions is less finely drawn now than at any time this century. It is not only Parliament which rubber-stamps decisions made elsewhere. Government departments themselves are often little more than passive spectators in a duel between competing groups; they, like Parliament, must accept the outcome with as good a grace as they can muster. In 1977 the Department of Prices and Consumer Protection was as powerless as Parliament to force a reduction in bread prices, given the opposition of those who made and those who delivered bread to the shops. More recently, neither Parliament nor Whitehall has been able to prohibit the advertisement of tobacco products, in the face of opposition from the powerful and deep-pocketed tobacco lobby. Nor, against an unholy alliance of religious, commercial and trade-union groups, have the Houses of Parliament or the Home Office felt able to legislate or propose legislation to allow shoppers to choose whether or not they wish to shop on Sunday as on any other day of the week.

The very liberality of constitutional norms which allows pressure groups to operate so freely as part of the British governing process has thus led, by stages, to a situation in which certain groups (which may or may not be representative, and whose leaders may or may not be democratically elected or accountable) appear to exercise a veto over particular areas of public administration. This itself would be cause enough for grave anxiety. But the anxieties go deeper than this. For very often this veto is surreptitious and hidden from public view.

At the political level, it may not be possible to know to what extent groups are partisan, and what politically-partisan influence they may have at Westminster. Groups which appear to be 'above' party politics are sometimes well immersed in political intrigue. In October 1981 Mrs Nancy Trenaman, in a report commissioned by the government into the activities of the Schools Council, singled out the Council's 'application of power politics to a matter so important as school education' for special criticism (*The Times*, 17 Oct. 1981:3). Two months later the poverty charity War on Want was publicly reprimanded by the Chief Charity Commissioner, Mr Terence FitzGerald, for indulging in activities (relating to unemployment in Britain) which carried party political overtones because of implicit emphasis upon Labour Party support (*The Times*, 3 Dec. 1981:6).

One can readily sympathise with the dilemma many pressure-group leaders find themselves in. To appeal to as wide an audience as possible a group must appear non-partisan. But to achieve goals, particularly in the context of Westminster or the local town hall, a group must play a political game. More often than not, playing politics means playing party politics. A group which desperately wishes to be, and to be seen to be, above politics may therefore find itself, almost imperceptibly, forced off the neutral cross-benches.

In 1975 the Police Federation took the unprecedented step of launching a campaign for 'law and order'. It claimed that there was nothing 'political' about crime, and that it had a right to comment on matters of public and parliamentary concern which affected the lives of its members. In 1978 the campaign was relaunched deliberately to influence the 1979 general election. 'We are anxious', Federation secretary Jim Jardine admitted, 'to make it a big election issue'; but he declared that the Federation would not become involved 'in campaigning on behalf of any party' (Reiner 1982). As the election approached, however, it became clear that there was remarkable similarity between Federation statements on law and order and those put out by Conservative politicians. A fortnight before polling, Metropolitan Police Commissioner Sir Robert Mark achieved a certain notoriety by publicly comparing the relationship between the Labour Party and the trade unions to 'the way the National Socialist German Workers' party achieved unrestricted control of the German state'. The following day most national newspapers carried a large advertisement placed by the Federation, blaming government (by implication, of course, Labour government) policies for rising crime rates (*Daily Telegraph*, 20 Apr. 1979:8 and 12). When the new Conservative government was installed the Federation broke with past practice, which had been that its parliamentary adviser had been drawn from the opposition party, and reappointed the Conservative MP Eldon Griffiths. The Federation has thus, despite its protestations to the contrary, become politicized in a way which would have seemed unimaginable twenty years ago. The policies of the Conservative Party, in relation both to police pay and to law and order, are so much nearer than those of Labour to the present mood of the Federation's members, that it is difficult to see how such a politicization could have been avoided.

Indulging in politics usually means taking sides. Where a pressure group has contractual relationships with MPs, even with MPs from more than one party, taking sides can hardly be avoided, because the MPs so retained are bound to be seen in an adversarial light. The relationship between MPs and pressure groups is a delicate area, in which the present arrangements are widely regarded as unsatisfactory. It is simply not possible to determine publicly whether a Member of Parliament is speaking on behalf of or has any connection with a particular group. It is true that in July 1975 the House of Commons, by resolution, set up a Register of Members' Interests. But the Register is a voluntary one, in two respects. Firstly, MPs do not have to register at all. Mr Enoch Powell, Ulster Unionist MP for South Down, has consistently refused to do so, arguing that only an Act of Parliament can oblige an MP to register; latterly the Rev. Ian Paisley, Democratic Unionist MP for North Antrim, has declined to declare his interests on the register, as have the Conservative MPs Sir John Langford-Holt and Kenneth Lewis and the Labour MP Alex Lyon (Rush 1981). In 1976 the Select Committee on Members' Interests proposed to the House that a new standing order should be passed, allowing the Committee to report to the House when a Member had refused to file an entry declaring his interests, and to recommend that the offending MP should be suspended; no action has yet been taken on these proposals.

Secondly, MPs who do register (the overwhelming majority) are solely responsible for their own entries. No independent check is made on the veracity or completeness of these entries. This is a particularly grave flaw in view of the fact that some Members of Parliament are not remunerated directly by organizations whose interests they represent, but indirectly through public relations companies; the apparent client is not the real one. As recently as 1977 it was demonstrated that seventy-eight MPs were 'consultants' on parliamentary matters to outside organizations or companies (Gillard and Tomkinson 1980:302). But much of this information remains hidden from public view.

The problems raised by public relations and parliamentary consultants are discussed below. Here we may note that the argument is by no means academic. The conviction for bribery, in February

1974, of the architect John Poulson opened to the public gaze a web of deceit and corruption which touched Parliament itself. A Select Committee of the Commons set up in 1976 to investigate the involvement of certain MPs in the Poulson case found that John Cordle, MP for Bournmouth East, had committed a contempt of Parliament; he was forced to resign his seat. Two other MPs were named by the Select Committee as having behaved in a way which the Committee felt was inconsistent with the standards the House of Commons was entitled to expect from its Members. It was later revealed that one of these MPs, the former Conservative Minister Reginald Maudling, only escaped prosecution for corruption *because* he was a Member of Parliament (*The Times*, 22 Oct. 1981:4). For it is an astonishing fact that, neither under the Public Bodies Corrupt Practices Act of 1889 nor under the Prevention of Corruption Act of 1906, can a Member of Parliament be held liable for prosecution for corruption; a Member simply does not fall under any of the existing definitions of persons who may become liable.

One result of this state of affairs is as follows: when a private Bill is before Parliament a Member must declare any pecuniary interest, and cannot vote on the measure. The House of Commons would be within its rights in requiring the sponsors of a private Bill to disclose the names of all MPs with such an interest; in March 1981 the Speaker advised the fifty-three MPs who were members of Lloyd's to refrain from voting on the Bill, then before Parliament, to reform the structure and powers of the famous underwriting society (*The Times*, 25 Mar. 1981:17). But when a public Bill or other matter is before Parliament, although MPs are supposed (in line with a resolution of the Commons passed in May 1974) to declare their interests when they speak in a debate or in proceedings related to such interests, there is really no way of knowing whether this rule is being adhered to. A civil servant or local councillor who accepted a bribe in order to use his position to influence the course of legislation would be guilty of corruption, in respect of which there are severe criminal penalties. But a Member of Parliament who accepted a bribe to the same end would – unless found out – escape scotfree; and even if found out, no criminal penalties would accrue.

The revelations of the Poulson affair indicate that it is far from fanciful to suggest that an MP might be tempted to act in such a manner. It is therefore perfectly possible and, indeed, relatively easy for a Member to receive from a pressure group payments designed to affect his parliamentary actions, without public anxiety being aroused. Perhaps this does not happen very often. It ought not to happen at all. It could be stopped by legislation preventing MPs from holding substantial outside interests while they sit in Parliament. But if this is thought draconian, and impracticable, there is no reason why the listing of interests in the Register of Members' Interests should not become obligatory and why the refusal to file a return to the Register should not lead to automatic suspension from Parliament. Those who elect a Member to Westminster have a right to know, beyond any reasonable doubt, the other interests their Member represents. At the same time it seems more than a little odd that while local councillors who fail to disclose financial interests should be subject to criminal penalties, MPs should be above the anti-corruption laws. There is a loophole here that needs tightening up without delay.

But if the possibility that MPs may act as advocates for secret interests gives grounds for disquiet, the activities of public relations firms and parliamentary consultants cause real worry. How much of this is justified? The Labour MP Robert Cryer has declared that some lobbying activities come close to 'subverting the democratic process'. In introducing his Registration of Commercial Lobbying Interests Bill into the House of Commons in February 1982 Mr Cryer argued that 'nobody should be able to buy influence in the House or in the machinery of Government' (HC *Debates*, 2 February 1982: col. 127). Had it become law his Bill would have required the establishment of a public register of 'all companies, sole traders or partnerships who seek to organize the lobbying of Parliament to try to influence the course of legislation or its application as their sole major commercial purpose'. Such organizations would have been obliged to file lists of all clients and meetings with ministers and civil servants, and to provide statements of all expenses and commissions, including fees and expenses paid to MPs.

One can agree with all of this without necessarily accepting Mr Cryer's premise that commercial lobbying agencies 'buy influence' or subvert the constitution. The Public Relations Consultants Association (PRCA), founded in 1969, has made valiant efforts to introduce a register of firms engaged in public relations and consultancy. Membership of the PRCA is subject to compliance with a strict and publicly available Code of Consultancy Practice, enforced by a disciplinary committee. Some of the elements of this Code are worth quoting in full:

3. A member firm shall cause all its clients to be listed in the Annual Register of the Public Relations Consultants Association.

4. A member firm shall cause all its directors, executives and retained consultants who hold public office, are members of either House of Parliament, are members of local authorities or of any statutory organization or body, to be recorded in the relevant sections of the Annual Register of the Public Relations Consultants Association.
8. A member firm shall not propose to clients any action which would constitute an improper influence on organs of government or legislation.
11. A member firm shall not purport to serve some announced cause while actually serving an undisclosed special or private interest.

The Annual Register of the PRCA is contained in the *Public Relations Yearbook*, published by Financial Times Business Publishing in co-operation with the Association. For each member company the Register gives a full list of its clients, a list of its subsidiary and associate companies, details of the company's partners and directors, and a separate list of all directors, partners or consultants who hold public office. Thus, under 'Political Research & Communication International Limited', clients listed (1982) include the Motor Cycle Association of Great Britain, the National Bus Company and Kentucky Fried Chicken; holder of public office associated with the company include the Conservative MPs Peter Fry (the company's chairman) and William Whitlock, as well as Douglas Smith, a councillor of the London Borough of Haringey, who is also a director of the company. The entry for 'Communications Strategy Limited' reveals that its clients include the Association of British Launderers & Cleaners, the Association of Sanitary Protection Manufacturers, and the Dry Cleaning Information Bureau, and that it retains as parliamentary consultant the Conservative MP Tim Brinton. The entry for 'Paul Winner Marketing Communications Limited' shows that its clients include the Conservation Society and the Malcolm Sargent Cancer Fund for Children and that its chairman, Paul Winner, is a Justice of the Peace.

The PRCA's Register is an impressive document. But it has a number of drawbacks deriving from the fact that inclusion in it, like membership of the PRCA itself, is purely voluntary. The 1982 *Yearbook* lists 200 companies, but of these only 100 (representing, it is true, about three-quarters of the industry's annual turnover) are members of the Association, entitled to call themselves Registered Public Relations Consultants and bound by the Code of Consultancy Practice. The remaining companies have agreed to provide information to the *Financial Times* as a condition of inclusion in the *Yearbook*, but are not bound by the Code nor by the requirements necessary for membership of the Association, such as a confidential declaration of fee income. More seriously, some of the leading firms working in the field of parliamentary consultancy are not listed at all. Camden Consultants, which has acted on behalf of the Pools Promoters Association and British Rail, is not in the *Yearbook*. Nor is Lloyd-Hughes Associates, whose remarkable claims were detailed in Chapter 3, and whose activities were extensively referred to by Mr Cryer when he introduced his Bill.

One can only speculate upon the reasons which have induced some firms to decline to be listed in the *Yearbook*; unwillingness to reveal lists of clients is certainly a factor, as is refusal to disclose fee income. So although the PRCA must be applauded for its efforts to shed more light on the world of parliamentary consultancies, it is clear that the voluntary system it operates is not satisfactory, because a compulsory register of lobbying interests and a compulsory register of MPs' interests are really two sides of the same coin. A number of solutions suggest themselves. One is to adopt Mr Cryer's proposal, or something based upon it, echoing the provisions (but not the weaknesses) of the Federal Regulation of Lobbying Act of 1946, which requires all lobbyists in Washington to register with Congress and to file quarterly returns showing details of their expenditure (Truman 1971:527). A second solution would be to invest the PRCA with much greater powers than it has at present. It would be possible to make membership of the PRCA obligatory for all public relations consultants, in the same way that membership of the Pharmaceutical Society is obligatory for all pharmaceutical chemists. This would probably be more acceptable to the public relations industry; it would also be cheaper.

To make these criticisms of the present state of affairs is, however, a far cry from accepting the wilder accusations levelled at professional lobbyists in Britain. Pressure groups are part of the democratic process. They no more subvert that process by employing professional parliamentary consultants to get a particular message across at Westminster or Whitehall than do trade unions by sponsoring and making payments to MPs, or organizations such as the Police Federation by having a Member of Parliament as a parliamentary adviser. If corrupt practices are indulged in, this is of course entirely wrong; there are laws to deal with them, though it would be helpful if these laws touched MPs as fully as they do ordinary citizens. But occurrences of bribery and corruption are not likely to be frequent; the point about the Poulson affair is that Poulson, and those associated with him, were found out.

Parliamentary consultants are brokers. They act as advocates for their clients in much the same way as solicitors or barristers present cases in courts. They spend a great deal of time just meeting people, listening as well as talking. A pressure group could lobby on its own behalf; many do so. Others, particularly those unversed in the ways of British government or not fortunate enough to have acquired the services of an MP or ex-MP or an 'honorary research assistant' to an MP, save themselves a good deal of time, and probably money, by employing professional assistance. It must also be remembered that although MPs and civil servants may listen to what lobbyists and pressure groups have to say, they are under no obligation to be convinced by what they hear. The most damning criticism of parliamentary consultants, apart from the secrecy which shrouds the activities of some of them, is that their services cost money: that only wealthy clients can afford to employ them. Basically this is true, though some campaigns are remarkably cheap; one, mentioned in Chapter 3, which was completely successful cost the client less than £300. It is perhaps conceivable that a system, akin to the legal aid service or that provided by citizens' advice bureaux, might be instituted, by which poor pressure groups could receive subsidized advice and help from professional lobbyists, on the basis of a test of means. There are, after all, far worse ways of spending public money. For the moment, however, differential access to professional lobbyists on account of the cost involved is indeed (to use the words of a senior civil servant to the author) 'the way of the world'. But it does not, objectively viewed, appear to be an issue worthy of great public agitation. The same cannot be said of the relationship between pressure groups and the organs of central government. In this relationship are to be found some of the activities to which the description 'subversive' would only be a slight exaggeration. To understand why this is so, it is helpful to outline one or two campaigns carried out by pressure groups at governmental level.

The success of the Birmingham Chamber of Commerce in persuading the Board of Trade to approve, with financial support from the government, a new Exhibition Centre in Birmingham rather than in London, is not atypical. Briefly, during the late 1960s an intense rivalry developed between Birmingham and London as the site for a national exhibition centre. At first sight Birmingham's chances appeared hopeless. The Birmingham Chamber of Commerce had to contend with opposition from the Greater London Council, the Society of Motor Manufacturers and Traders, the Association of Exhibition Organizers, the Confederation of British Industry, the British National Export Council, the City of London and a host of other London-orientated interests. Although Birmingham was, admittedly, at the centre of one of the country's most important manufacturing regions, there were many who questioned the wisdom of siting a *national* exhibition centre on the outskirts of a city 100 miles from the nation's capital. But the Birmingham Chamber of Commerce knew how to supplicate in the right place; its officials were tireless in their efforts to persuade a small group of Whitehall decision-makers of the strength of Birmingham's case. In January 1970 the President of the Board of Trade, Roy Mason, announced that the government had approved the Birmingham proposal, promising, into the bargain, £1.5 millions from public funds to aid the project; this decision was confirmed by the incoming Conservative administration the following July. There had been no public discussion of the matter, and no feasibility study of the alternatives (*The Times*, 14 July 1970:17 and 23).

The story of the campaign to establish commercial television in Britain reveals the same tendency to government by stealth (H. H. Wilson 1961). The Television Act of 1954 established commercial television, financed by advertising revenue, in competition with the BBC, whose monopoly was therefore broken. The inauguration of commercial television conflicted with the recommendations of the majority report of the Beveridge Committee on Broadcasting (1947–49) and had not been mentioned in the 1951 Conservative election manifesto. There is little evidence that the public was much interested in the idea, and most members of the Cabinet were unenthusiastic. But the advertising fraternity, aided and abetted by a number of finance houses and sections of the television and electrical industries, set to work with a will to convince backbench Conservative MPs that commercial television was good for the nation. In July 1953 a Popular Television Association was formed with the object of creating an apparently 'spontaneous' public outcry against the continuation of the BBC's monopoly; this campaign included propaganda disguised as news stories, inspired letters to the press, as well as pamphlets and lectures. Conservative Central Office was won over to the cause. The Cabinet capitulated and the Act was passed.

Now it is probably true that the BBC monopoly of television was not in the national interest. In the author's personal opinion the establishment of commercial television has enriched the life of the nation as well as the bank accounts of independent television contractors and shareholders. But the successful campaign for commercial television demonstrated that it is possible to effect a fundamental change in the British way of life, and to dispose of considerable national assets, without any form of serious public debate and certainly without any form of public approval (Jay 1970). Lord Hailsham, who led a spirited resistance to the measure, declared with some justification that the passage of the 1954 Act, despite the omission from the 1951 Conservative manifesto of any possibility of introducing commercial television, was 'a shoddy and squalid constitutional error' (quoted in H. H. Wilson, 1961:194). So it was. It is no defence of the Popular Television Association to claim that it was the government and Parliament which passed the Act, and that the pressure group involved had clean hands; it originated this particular subversion of the democratic process and it must share the blame.

Pressure groups can create public opinion where there is none to be found and, by concentrating upon the small elite of decision-makers that rules the country, are able to affect the deployment or redeployment of national resources without reference to the general will. Democracy is by-passed. Worse than this, however, democracy can be fooled. Not all pressure groups are what they seem. The National Smoke Abatement Society, forerunner of the National Society for Clean Air, derived financial support from manufacturers of smokeless fuels and the Solid Smokeless Fuels Federation (Sanderson 1974:28). In the mid-1960s the London Foundation for Marriage Education and the Genetic Study Unit both campaigned against the use of oral contraceptives and extolled the virtues of mechanical, and in particular of rubber, contraceptive aids. Both organizations were, according to Professor Wootton, the creation of London Rubber Industries, Britain's largest manufacturer of rubber contraceptives, who were no doubt anxious to stem the growing popularity of the contraceptive pill (Wootton 1978:165).

In trying to unravel the mysteries of a campaign for rubber contraceptive devices, however, we do at least have the consolation of knowing that the campaign itself, irrespective of who was actually behind it, was and had to be public. So it is with the examples given earlier. A national exhibition centre cannot be built *secretly* on the outskirts of Birmingham, nor can a commercial television network be launched without the public knowing something about it. Even to be wise after the event is preferable to not being wise at all. But there are instances of campaigns being conducted almost entirely in secret; only the alertness of a Fleet Street reporter, or a breach of confidence by a disgruntled civil servant, has allowed the public to know anything at all about what has been going on. In August 1981 the British government announced, without any prior public warning, that, with effect from 1 September 1981, it was going to prohibit the importation into the United Kingdom of raw poultry reared in countries whose policy it was to vaccinate poultry against Newcastle disease (a form of fowl pest) rather than to slaughter infected birds. France was one such country, and the effect of the British government's sudden decision was to prevent the British Christmas turkey market from being flooded with frozen French turkeys, which were cheaper. There was no obvious veterinary justification for the action of the British government. British turkey breeders were overjoyed. The National Farmers' Union did not disguise its pleasure at the new regulations. But British consumers were less happy. Why had Parliament not been asked for its views? Where had the representations come from which had led to this unexpected change in poultry policy? No one outside the privileged circle of the Ministry of Agriculture and the farmers' lobby was ever told.*

In short, some interests do appear to be able to exert powerful and compelling influences upon government practically without let or hindrance, and, more especially, without opposing interests being given an adequate opportunity of expressing a contrary view. Even where there is what is termed 'wide consultation', the manner in which that consultation is carried out is not always satisfactory. The author has seen a copy of an internal minute written in February 1982 by a senior civil servant in one of the great departments of state, setting out the terms of a draft letter and discussion paper to be sent to interested parties concerning a matter that was to come before an advisory committee. The civil servant drew a distinction between those organizations that were to be consulted and invited to comment upon the matter under discussion, and those that were merely to be informed of it; in relation to one organization the writer of the minute confessed that he was unsure whether it ought to be on either list, but he included it in the latter. Now there can be no doubt that this senior civil servant was acting in absolute good faith, and with great integrity, in compiling the two lists. Copies of the draft letter and discussion paper were, additionally, placed in the Libraries of the House of Commons and the House of Lords. So there was no question here of secret government. Equally, however, there is no doubt that the two lists represented, at any rate in relation to the matter under discussion, two levels of group contact, two league tables which the department had compiled. The discussion docu-

*On 15 July 1982 the Court of Justice of the European Communities ruled that the British poultry ban imposed on 1 September 1981 was illegal (*The Times*, 26 July 1982:4).

ment was not communicated to the press. If an interested group was not on either list its opportunities to comment on the matter in question were virtually non-existent.

The difficulties discussed here relate partly to the wider issue of open government, and some of them could be met very easily, given the political will. Whenever a Bill or Statutory Instrument is presented to Parliament, or a White Paper is published, it does not seem revolutionary to ask that there should be made publicly available lists of those individuals and organizations whose views and representations have been canvassed or considered, regardless of whether they have been adopted. Such lists could be attached to the Bill, Statutory Instrument or White Paper in exactly the same way that government departments are obliged to attach 'Explanatory Notes' to Statutory Instruments which they sponsor. Such a modest reform would have a further impact, which touches upon a more basic difficulty which the activities of pressure groups pose for the working of democracy. Given that pressure groups are here to stay, and that their activities form part of the warp and weft of decision-making in British government, questions of representativeness and accountability must be considered. When a pressure group launches a campaign, makes representations to the government or pronounces on an issue of public concern, on whose behalf and in whose name is it actually speaking?

Again, some examples will make this point very clear. The Automobile Association and the Royal Automobile Club are continually in dialogue with the Department of Transport on motoring matters, and their opinions are accepted by the Department, and by the media, as representing the views of motorists (Starkie 1982:46). 'Because of its large membership', the Association's annual report for 1963 boasted, 'the AA is able to speak with authority on behalf of motorists as a whole and is regarded both by central and by local government as a powerful and responsible influence in motoring affairs' (quoted in Plowden 1971:373). Now it is certainly the case that, between them, membership of these two motoring organizations accounts for over half of the car-owning population of the United Kingdom. But they really cannot be said to 'represent' the motoring public. 'Full members' of the Royal Automobile Club are members of Automobile Proprietary Ltd., a holding company whose board of directors they elect. But motorists who 'join' the RAC in order to obtain motoring services (provided by a subsidiary company) are merely associate members. The Club does have an Associate Committee, but its rights appear to be consultative only, and those on it who can claim to represent individual associate members amount to only one quarter of its membership; they are, moreover, chosen from a larger body of twenty members *selected* by the Club's General Council. The structure of the AA is in theory more democratic. Its affairs are controlled and managed by a committee elected by members, and one quarter of the committee is elected at each Annual General Meeting, which all AA members are eligible to attend. But no member who is not already on the committee is eligible for election to it unless his nomination is approved by three-quarters of the committee; and no particular quorum for the holding of an Annual General Meeting is required.

Now, to point out that neither the Automobile Association no the Royal Automobile Club has a structure which may be regarde as truly democratic is not to decry or belittle the many valuabl services they perform. Moreover, it must in fairness be stated tha there is little evidence to suggest that motorists who subscribe t either organization are in revolt against the oligarchies who, in prac tice, control them. Nonetheless, the willingness of government t entertain perpetual dialogues with manifestly unrepresentati groups is clearly evidenced in the case of the AA and the RAC, and to be found in many other spheres. The Home Office and the Min try of Agriculture regard the Board of Deputies of British Jews as t representative organ of Anglo-Jewry. Yet the Board of Deput does not represent individual Jews, only Jewish communal organi tions, some of which are little more than rotten boroughs. 'One J (or Jewess) one vote' is not a precept which holds for the election the Deputies, so that multiple voting is commonplace. The Board Deputies represents primarily a self-perpetuating elite of Angl Jewish leaders, intent on articulating the opinions of the Angl Jewish community at Westminster and Whitehall. The Metropolit Police and the Home Office treat with the Licensed Taxi Driver Association as representing the London taxi trade; in fact, out about 17,000 licensed taxi-drivers in the Greater London area th Association can only claim to represent about 4,500 (*The Times*, Nov. 1980:4).

A subsidiary but not unimportant consideration in connectio with the representativeness of pressure groups is the problem o multiple membership. Many motorists belong *both* to the AA *and* to the RAC. Many people concerned with the environment belong to the National Trust, the Council for the Protection of Rural England, the Civic Trust, the Ramblers' Association, and so on. A campaign supported by all these environmental groups appears very powerful. But how many *individuals* are actually represented? In his study of the controversy that raged in the mid 1960s over proposals to build a reservoir at Cow Green, in Upper Teesdale, Professor Roy Gregory has drawn attention to the way in which 'through their multiple and interlocking memberships and affiliations, a small but dedicated group of energetic people may be able to activate centres of opposition across a whole range of institutions' (Gregory 1971:60). A key role in the organization of opposition to the Cow Green scheme was played by Dr Margaret Bradshaw, a Staff Tutor in Botany in the Extra-Mural Department of the University of Durham; according to Professor Gregory, Dr Bradshaw was associated with no less than six organizations concerned with environmental and ecological issues. A number of other individuals who led the protests were, simultaneously, members of the Council for the Protection of Rural England, the Ramblers' Association, the Youth Hostels Association and the Botanical Society. Partly through multiple membership of this sort, a small number of dedicated objectors were able to mobilize a dozen or so learned societies and environmental bodies of the highest repute. To point this out is not to detract in any way from the righteousness of their cause or from the selfless dedication with which they fought for it. The battle for Cow Green (the reservoir scheme was approved by Parliament in 1967) does however serve as a reminder that 'widespread opposition' may not be all it seems at first sight.

How is a democracy to cope with this situation? Civil servants answer that they have to deal with *someone*, and that representativeness is in any case relative. Perhaps it is. The major question here is one of *public* accountability. Most pressure groups are accountable to those who finance and participate in them, though, as the example of the RAC shows, even this is not always the case. But this is private accountability. There does seem to be a need, in addition to a compulsory register of lobbying organizations, for unrestricted public access to certain basic information about all pressure groups, including (a) their sources of finance, (b) their certified membership figures, (c) their own internal constitutional arrangements or articles of association, (d) their formal links with other groups, (e) their office holders, and (f) their expenditure, including payments made to public relations firms, MPs, local councillors and the media, The task of collating such information and of making it available to the public might be given to a registrar, modelled on the Registrar of Friendly Societies, to whom might also be allotted the task of maintaining a register of lobbyists.

The foregoing criticisms of the institutional framework within which pressure groups operate are made in a constructive spirit, and in the conviction that since much public policy is the outcome of pressure-group interaction, this is a healthy and not a sinister development, and deserves to be encouraged. It remains now to consider some of the wider issues raised by the participation of pressure groups in modern British government. This consideration is premissed upon the view that Britain is now a corporative state. The government of the country is a partnership between the private and the public sectors, between government (Whitehall moderated by Westminster) and private interests. At the economic level this is easy to recognize. The National Economic Development Council, established in 1961, is a forum where the government shares with management and workers (represented by the Confederation of British Industry and the Trades Union Congress) the job of marrying economic plans for the nation to the available resources. In 1974 the Manpower Services Commission came into existence, and had transferred to it many of the tasks previously performed by the Department of Employment; it is a partnership between the Trades Union Congress, the Confederation of British Industry, local authority and educational interests groups, and is staffed by civil servants. The Health and Safety Executive, created by Act of Parliament in 1974, is run on similar lines.

But what might be termed functional corporatism extends beyond the economic and industrial sectors. Agricultural policy is a partnership between the Ministry of Agriculture and the National Farmers' Union. Educational policy is the outcome of government thinking, voiced by the Department of Education and Science, modified and refined by inputs from a wide variety of educational, local authority and religious bodies. Transport policy emerges from an amalgam of road and rail lobbies, industrial concerns and environmental groups. The growth of functional corporatism has been accompanied by an increasing tendency for those outside government to be 'seconded' for limited periods to government departments, and for civil servants to spend some time working in industry or commerce (Richardson and Jordan 1979:63–5). On the face of it the cross-fertilization of ideas which result from such moves is surely to be encouraged. But two particular aspects give grounds for legitimate worry.

The first concerns the safeguarding of the interests of the state, and of the taxpayers' money, when a civil servant or ex-Minister accepts a business or other outside appointment. In two papers commissioned by the Select Committee of the House of Commons on the

Treasury and Civil Service, Professor Robert Vaughan, of the American University, Washington DC, pointed out that such postings could lead to the improper use of confidential information by the employing body, and might enable that body to exert undue influence upon a government department or agency. Even if no improper use of information is made, or no undue influence exerted, the suspicion that public policy was being affected thereby might undermine public confidence (*The Times*, 7 July 1980:4).

Secondly, it is undeniable that any organization which attracts into its employ a Minister or civil servant from the government department with which it has had most dealings, must be at an advantage. The new employee will be someone who 'knows his way around', who is almost certainly on first-name terms with the decision-makers in that department, and who knows its weaknesses and blind spots. The tendency for ex-civil servants and former Ministers to take up positions of importance with representative organizations has been increasing significantly over the past couple of decades. Something of the impact such appointments have may be gauged from an extract from the late Richard Crossman's diaries, referring to an application (never, as it happens, followed through) made in November 1969 by Sir Clifford Jarrett, Permanent Under-Secretary at the Department of Health and Social Security, to take up on his retirement a post as President of the Corporation of Society of Pension Consultants; the Head of the Home Civil Service had already given his permission. Crossman, the Secretary of State, had other ideas (Crossman, 1977:732; 745):

> I am sure there is nothing dishonest about it . . . but in the following three years all the important decisions will be taken about its [the Superannuation Bill's] application, and he will be there to look after their [the pension consultants'] interests.
>
> * * * *
>
> I really don't want to have him as my Permanent Secretary if he is negotiating with the enemy about crossing the line as soon as he leaves the Department.

The effect of such an appointment is, without doubt, to give the pressure group a distinct and subtle benefit in its dealings with government. M. J. Barnett, in his study of rent legislation, draws attention to the importance attached by the Ministry of Housing to a memorandum drafted by Harold Symon, who had in 1955 moved from the Ministry, where he had been an under-secretary, to the position of director of the Association of Land and Property Owners, a landlords' pressure group (Barnett 1969:17). 'It was', comments Professor Barnett, 'the capacity to influence decisions before they were taken that in this as in most legislation constituted a significant advantage' (Barnett 1969:22). Symon's former position meant that he commanded the close attention of civil servants in the Ministry, who were prepared to accord his views a degree of respect quite above that given to the policies of other bodies.

Of course the movement is not all in one direction. There are instances of recruitment from pressure groups to government departments (Richardson and Jordan 1979:69). But such examples are comparatively rare, whereas those of movement from government to pressure groups are not. Richardson and Jordan list seventeen examples since 1955, and another twelve are referred to by Professor Wootton (Richardson and Jordan 1979:66–7; Wootton 1978:192). While the appointment of an ex-Minister or an ex-civil servant to a pressure group does not necessarily subvert the democratic process, the risk that it may have this result is always present. In the case of civil servants the risk is to some extent already recognized. The *Civil Service Pay and Conditions Code* (para. 9961) lays down the rule that all civil servants of the rank of Under-Secretary (or, in the Diplomatic Service, Counsellors) and above, and of the equivalent ranks in the armed forces, are required to obtain the consent of the government before accepting, within two years of resignation or retirement, offers of employment in business and other bodies, particularly those with which the government is in 'a special relationship'. This requirement also applies to posts of a special or technical nature below the rank of Under-Secretary.

Some comments need to be made about this rule. The first is that the period of two years within which permission must be sought is certainly not long enough. The time during which an issue can remain 'live' in a department can be prolonged, and is rarely less than two years except in the most minor and routine matters; five years would seem a safer period of 'quarantine' for ex-civil servants before they are allowed, without permission, to take up posts with outside bodies. The second observation is that the present regulation contains an obvious loophole, for it talks about 'offers of employment'. Now it is perfectly possible to give one's services to an organization without being employed by it; a person who established himself as a one-man company, to which a lobby, or business or trade union turned for advice on a fee-paying basis, would not be in that body's employment. Thirdly, what holds for civil servants ought surely to hold for government Ministers. At present an Advisory Committee on Business Appointments makes recommendations to the Prime Minister on applications from Permanent Secretaries and Second Permanent Secretaries in the civil service, and from those of equivalent rank in the armed forces, who wish to accept business appointments after resignation or retirement. But the Advisory Committee does not advise on matters relating to Ministers. There seems no good reason why the rules, however inadequate, which apply to civil servants should not also apply to those politically in control of government departments. The present purely voluntary arrangement by which ex-Ministers seek guidance on the acceptance of business appointments needs to be placed on a much firmer footing, preferably by statute. Finally, if there is already compulsory vetting of applications by ex-civil servants (albeit only for twenty-four months after retirement or resignation), and voluntary vetting of applications by ex-Ministers, why cannot lists be published of the fate of all these applications? As with many of the other worries generated by the activities of pressure groups, a little publicity in this area would work wonders.

Beyond this, the major concerns which are from time to time expressed about the impact of pressure groups upon the process of government seem largely unfounded. That a pressure group succeeds in its objective, that a campaign is crowned with victory, is not in itself a cause for concern; many campaigns deserve to be successful. Without pressure groups the Corn Laws would not have been repealed, the Factory Acts would not have been passed, the activities, even the existence, of trade unions would never have been legalized, and some of the most important social and environmental reforms of the post-1945 period would never have seen the light of day. It is still fashionable in some circles to contrast 'sectional interests' with 'the national interest'; and thus to castigate pressure groups because it is alleged they represent the former, in contradistinction (and, by inference, in opposition) to the latter. This comparison is false not least because it is based upon a fundamental misunderstanding of modern British parliamentary democracy. It is the business of government, and of the organs of government, to do what the citizens of the state want, not what it is thought is in their interests. In a democracy it is the *wishes* of the people, not their interests (defined by whom?) which are paramount. Naturally, if a pressure group distorts the wishes of the people, or frustrates the implementation of those wishes, then that activity is truly pernicious. But insofar as a pressure group expresses the real wishes of a section of the population, however small, it is an asset to a democratic society.

It must be admitted at once that there are examples of pressure groups acting in a pernicious manner. The activities of the Popular Television Association in relation to the inauguration of commercial television, and of the Birmingham Chamber of Commerce in respect of the national exhibition centre, were hardly consistent with the maintenance of an open society. The campaign to abolish the death penalty for murder was fired with the deepest moral fervour and human idealism; but there can be no doubt that its success was achieved in the face of the opposition of a majority of British citizens, whose views were trampled underfoot when the 1965 Act was passed (Alderman 1978a:98; Pym 1974:106–7). Fortunately, however, such examples, though serious, are by no means widespread or abundant. By virtue of a species of Newtonian law of political dynamics, to *almost* every group there is an opposition group, though one not always equal in strength. The Trades Union Congress is matched by the Confederation of British Industry. Individual unions and trade councils are balanced by employers' associations and chambers of commerce. Every form of transport has representative groups for those who give, those who use and those who are affected by the service provided. Those who pollute the environment must contend with those who seek its protection. There are pro- and anti-smoking organizations (the Freedom Organization for the Right to Enjoy Smoking Tobacco, and Action on Smoking and Health). The brewing interests must contend with the National Council on Alcoholism and other bodies dedicated to the reduction of consumption of beer and spirits. Nor is this phenomenon of opposites confined to sectional groups. The League Against Cruel Sports, an anti-hunting body, is openly opposed by the British Shooting Sports Council. The Legalise Cannabis Campaign must contend with a powerful and, at the moment, dominant lobby opposed to its ideas.

These opposites do not necessarily balance each other. To the inherent relative weakness of some groups compared with others there are external factors to consider: for example, differential access to the media. No pressure group can be guaranteed a public hearing, and it is undoubtedly true that some groups, such as the campaign to legalize cannabis, have found it notoriously difficult to arrange advertising and public meetings or to obtain serious attention from the press, radio and television. It is also true that rich and powerful groups generally have a much easier time putting their views across, at all levels, than the poor and the weak. But this disparity is not as great now as it once was. A number of radio and television programmes are specially devoted to giving pressure groups a chance to air their views. Many cause groups are given free time to explain their aims and to appeal for funds, and it has become fashionable for well-known personalities to lend their names to such appeals; in April 1982, for instance, BBC Television screened an appeal by Lady Katherine Boyle on behalf of the Birds' Welfare and Protection Association. The 'Open Door' programme on BBC2 enables groups to present programmes with professional technical advice and at minimal cost. Even very small groups have learned how to harness the power of the television medium. In the summer of 1972, having failed by press publicity and complaints to persuade Buckinghamshire County Council to replace a bridge on a footpath linking two villages in the north of the county, a local footpath protection group staged a march for the benefit of a regional evening magazine programme on BBC television. Three weeks later a new bridge had been placed in position (Hall 1974:42).

In the past consumers' interests have been grossly under-represented at Westminster and Whitehall. This is no longer the case. There is now a Minister for Prices and Consumer Protection, a National Consumer Council and an Office of Fair Trading. Justice, the British Section of the International Commission of Jurists, devotes some of its considerable energies to the advancement of consumer interests and to the campaign to strengthen the hand of consumers, especially in the public sector (Wraith 1976). The Consumers' Association (founded October 1957), publisher of *Which?* magazine, has transformed the face of consumerism and can claim to its credit many political victories over vested industrial and business interests. As an example, in November 1981 it stepped into the dispute between the British car industry and motorists wishing to import cars from the Continent for their own personal use. Because car dealers in Britain add about 20 per cent to the cost of a car as their profit, whereas dealers in Common Market countries generally add only 10 per cent, British motorists who purchase cars on the Continent (even British-made cars) can save £1,000 or more, even after transport costs and the payment of car and value-added tax at the port of entry. British car manufacturers, and British importers of European cars, urged the Department of Transport to clamp down on this trade, by requiring that a car must be driven abroad for six months before it can classify as a personal import. The Consumers' Association retaliated by deliberately publishing a step-by-step guide to buying new cars in Common Market countries. The Department of Transport refused to act against this activity and implicitly condemned the British motor lobby for attempting to restrict imports of this nature.

Nor are consumers' interests always poor. The Campaign for Lead-Free Air ('CLEAR') was launched in January 1982 with funds of £63,000. It immediately embarked upon a nationwide media campaign, including a £10,000 advertisement in the *Observer* and a £1,000 poll carried out by a leading polling organization; the poll claimed to have found that nine out of ten people thought lead in petrol a health hazard. At the same time CLEAR leaked to *The Times* an interdepartmental letter, written by Sir Henry Yellowlees, chief medical officer of the Department of Health, which suggested that 'truly conclusive evidence' about the effects of lead pollution may be unobtainable' (*New Society*, 15 Apr. 1982:89). Within three months an all-party support group of 130 MPs had been formed. CLEAR has a full-time staff led by Des Wilson, formerly organizer of Shelter, the National Campaign for the Homeless. The Campaign for Lead-Free Air is thus neither a poor nor an amateur group. Its ability to generate media coverage has justly earned it the respect of the Department of Health as well as of car manufacturers and petrol companies.

We may also note that though the disparity between a rich and a poor group may be great, the rich do not always win. Sometimes, indeed, the very opulence of a vested interest can work to its disadvantage and to its ultimate undoing. Of this there is no better example than the battle over resale price maintenance (RPM) in 1964. In January of that year Edward Heath, then President of the Board of Trade, announced in the Commons that the Conservative government intended to legislate to prohibit (with certain exceptions) the system whereby manufacturers and wholesalers required retailers to abide by minimum price levels for the sale of their products. RPM had been under attack for some time, particularly from large retail chains and discount houses. In 1960 over thirty associations of manufacturers, wholesalers and retailers (especially small shopkeepers) had banded together to form the Resale Price Maintenance Co-ordinating Committee. The Committee indulged in astute lobbying within the ranks of the Conservative Party, and as soon as Mr Heath had made his announcement the Committee mounted a new offensive, rallying support at Westminster, appointing a public relations officer and a parliamentary agent. The National Chamber of Trade meanwhile called for mass rallies in Cardiff, Glasgow and London, and orchestrated a verbal assault upon the 1922 Committee of Conservative back benchers (*The Times*, 10 Feb. 1964:6).

This campaign had some success. When the House of Commons divided on the second reading of Mr Heath's Bill, over twenty Conservative MPs abstained and another twenty, in defiance of a three-line whip, voted against the measure. Because it was an election year the Labour opposition dared not oppose the Bill; but it did not wish to support it. At the committee and report stages, therefore, the government's majority was totally unpredictable; at one stage, on a division to exempt pharmaceutical products from the prohibition of RPM, the government's majority, normally 100, fell to one. Mr Heath had to make some important concessions on the status of existing RPM agreements (Bruce-Gardyne and Lawson 1976:80–118). But the Bill became law. Particularly because it was an election year, senior Conservative leaders were anxious that their party should not be seen to be defending the maintenance of price levels which were generally acknowledged to be artificially high. The Labour Party's decision to abstain was calculated to embarrass the government; but it was a decision that did not please many Labour backbenchers, to whom RPM generally smacked of the quite unacceptable face of monopolistic capitalism. In 1964 those organizations which spoke up for the consumer were very few. Mr Heath appeared as the champion of the poor and the weak. Though he had to make concessions he triumphed on the issue of principle, supported, it must be said, by a Board of Trade which had for some time put the abolition of RPM high on its list of economic priorities.

The battle over RPM demonstrates that the triumph of a powerful self-interested group over the public interest is neither automatic nor assured. But it also leads to two further observations concerning the dynamic impact of pressure groups on British government. In *The Governmental Process* David Truman argues that the dangers to democracy represented by the existence of groups have been much exaggerated, because the phenomena of 'overlapping membership' and 'potential interest groups' act as restraints. By 'overlapping membership' Truman means that no one individual in society has only one interest to pursue: a producer is also a consumer; a tax-payer is also a revenue-spender; a car manufacturer is also an inhaler of lead-polluted air. Translated to the group level this results in a given interest group containing within itself a diversity of aims and objectives, some of which will be shared with other and perhaps opposing groups. 'It is', says Truman, 'the competing claims of other groups *within* a given interest group that threaten its cohesion, and force it to reconcile its claims with those of other groups active on the political scene' (Truman 1971:510; see also Moodie and Studdert-Kennedy 1970:71–2). Although the lobby to retain RPM was very powerful, the Conservative Party, which was the object of its attentions, and to which some of its most influential protagonists belonged, also contained advocates of the free-market economy. Moreover, some manufacturers recognized that the abolition of RPM could lead (as it did) to increased sales, lower prices and hence greater turnover. One wing of the Labour Party was sympathetic to the survival of 'the small shopkeeper'; but another saw the effect upon standards of living of lower prices and rising industrial output. Overlapping membership thus ensured that though the lobby to retain RPM won some concessions it proved less powerful than the public interest expressed through the political parties.

By 'potential interest group' Truman means that any group which acts in society must recognize that its very existence may be a spur to the formation of an opposing group. The mere threat that such an opposing group may be formed will itself act as a restraining influence upon a group already in existence, and will give opposing interests some influence in the political process (Truman 1971:511). The more extreme demands of an existing group will therefore be curbed. In the case of the abolition of RPM the argument for the total preservation of RPM, without any modification, was never seriously put by more than a handful of MPs; rather, particular exemptions were argued on their merits. Had the Co-ordinating Committee set its face against *any* reform, it would rightly have been accused of pig-headed intransigence, and its stance would have invited the formation of a group dedicated to the state regulation of all retail prices. By the same token, the tobacco lobby has never been so rash as to claim that tobacco advertising should be free of all restraint, because such a claim would almost certainly result in statutory regulation; it has avoided this fate only by agreeing to voluntary restraint, however unsatisfactory others might feel this to be.

The history of the campaign to abolish RPM also illustrates very neatly what has been a central theme of this book: that public policy is for better or worse the outcome of pressure-group interaction. In any matter of public concern a variety of groups, organized and unorganized, will work to have their views adopted. There will be a policy outcome if one group is dominant or if several groups agree to compromise. But suppose two or more groups, of equal strength, remain obdurate? In that case no group will prevail.

This may not be in the national interest. In 1958 the late Professor R. T. McKenzie drew attention to the danger of 'pluralist stagnation' (McKenzie 1974:284). His fear has been echoed more recently by Professor S. H. Beer (Beer 1967:89–90). Put simply, pluralist, or pluralistic, stagnation is a state of affairs in which progress in society is stifled by a near-perfect balance of opposing group forces. It is not any particular group which threatens democracy, but the group *system*. A number of examples spring to mind. The North-West Essex and East Hertfordshire Preservation Association prevented Stansted from being developed as London's third airport. When it appeared that Cublington would be chosen instead, the Wing Airport Resistance Association swung into action, so that that option, too, had to be abandoned, this time in favour of Foulness. But even Foulness had its defenders, and was eventually abandoned as well. London's third airport has not yet been built. The issue of Sunday trading has never been resolved because the balance of competing interests is too delicate to upset the uneasy truce enshrined in the Sunday Trading Restriction Act of 1936; the provisions of that measure (now part of the 1950 Shops Act) are more honoured in the breach than in the observance, but they remain on the statute book. It has been argued that the entire history of attempts to pursue a successful incomes policy in Britain since 1945 has been dogged by pluralist stagnation, the trade unions being unable to prevent the introduction of such policies but strong enough to wreck them as and when they wish (Dorfman 1974:97). Professor Peter Hall, of Reading University, has voiced concern at the manner in which the mechanisms available for taking planning decisions in Britain appear to allow too much scope for objectors, with the result (in his view) that there is a paralysis of the planning process. He cites as an example the abandonment of plans to relieve traffic congestion in Greater London in the 1970s. The Labour administration then in charge of the Greater London Council bowed to pressure from the 'Homes Before Roads' lobby and did not go ahead with a scheme to construct a series of motorways around the metropolis. Later, plans for special lorry routes and extended bus-lanes were also dropped when they encountered determined opposition from local and sectional groups. The result, in Professor Hall's view, is that London has been left without a roads policy (*The Times*, 9 Apr. 1980:2).

Clearly, the charge of pluralist stagnation is not one that can be entirely or easily dismissed, as the above examples indicate. But, in common with the charge of subverting, or of coming close to subverting, the democratic process, it must be said of the relationship between pluralist stagnation and the activities of pressure groups that a few instances cannot sustain a blanket condemnation. Stagnation itself is a loaded word. At the end of the 1970s it was widely recognized that there was no urgency about London's need for a third airport; the 'stagnation' which resulted from the epic struggles of the different anti-airport groups thus saved the nation a great deal of unnecessary expenditure. And there are many people who really do believe in 'Homes Before Roads', and who argue that London is a healthier city without suburban motorways.

To say this is not to deny that the balance of pressure-group forces may frustrate any movement within the policy process. But against this risk must be weighed the enormous contribution which pressure groups make to the working of government. The democratic ideal does not begin and end at the ballot box, or in the party caucus. Participation in pressure groups enables large numbers of people (far larger than the million or so active in political parties) to involve themselves in decision-making processes *between* general elections; this, in its turn, is a wonderful corrective to the ability of governments to control the working of Parliament through the power of the party whips. But pressure groups accomplish more than this. The domination of British politics by political parties could result in the eclipse of many sensitive issues which are simply too controversial and divisive for the parties to handle. That such issues have been aired at all is due entirely to the existence of pressure groups.

If there are anomalies in the present first-past-the-post electoral system – as indeed there are – then the activities of pressure groups can help redress the balance. If the organs of central or of local government seem remote from the mass of the population – as indeed they can be – then participation within pressure groups can help restore a sense of participation in government. And if the complexities of modern society distance policy-makers from issues – as indeed they do – then the existence of pressure groups of all sorts can only serve to strengthen the governed against those who govern. This cannot but be for the public good.

REFERENCES AND BIBLIOGRAPHY

ALDERMAN, G. (1973) *The Railway Interest*, Leicester University Press.

ALDERMAN, G. (1978a) *British Elections: Myth & Reality*, Batsford.

ALDERMAN, G. (1978b) 'Fighters against the Front', *Jewish Chronicle*, 6 Oct.: 25.

ALDERMAN, G. (1982) 'Jews and Sunday trading: the use and abuse of delegated legislation', *Public Administration* x: 99–104.

ASHBY, E. & ANDERSON, M. (1981) *The Politics of Clean Air*, Oxford University Press.

BARNETT, M. J. (1969) *The Politics of Legislation. The Rent Act 1957*, Weidenfeld.

BEER, S. H. (1957) 'The representation of interests in British Government: historical background' *American Political Science Review* li: 614–27.

BEER, S. H. (1967) 'The British legislature and the problem of mobilizing consent' in *Essays on Reform*, 1967 (ed. B. Crick), Oxford University Press.

BEER, S. H. (1969) *Modern British Politics*, Faber.

BEITH, A. (1981) 'Prayers unanswered: a jaundiced view of the parliamentary scrutiny of statutory instruments', *Parliamentary Affairs* xxxiv: 165–73.

BELOFF, M. & PEELE, G. (1980) *The Government of the United Kingdom*, Weidenfeld.

BENTLEY, A. F. (1967) *The Process of Government* (ed. P. H. Odegard), Belknap Press.

BRADLEY, I. (1980) 'Pressure groups', *The Times*, 7, 8, 9 and 10 Apr.

BROOKES, S. K. & RICHARDSON, J. J. (1975) 'The Environmental Lobby in Britain', *Parliamentary Affairs* xxviii: 312–28.

BRUCE-GARDYNE, J. & LAWSON, N. (1976) *The Power Game*, Macmillan.

BURKE, E. (1823) *Works*, vol. III, Thomas M' Lean.
BUTLER, D. & KAVANAGH, D. (1979) *The British General Election of 1979*, Macmillan.
CAPON, J. (1972) *And There Was Light*, Lutterworth Press.
CASTLE, B. (1973) 'Mandarin Power', *Sunday Times*, 10 June: 17.
CHRISTOPH, J. B. (1962) *Capital Punishment and British Politics*, Allen & Unwin.
CLIFF, D. (1979) 'Religion, morality and the middle class' in *Respectable Rebels* (ed. R. King & N. Nugent), Hodder & Stoughton.
COHEN, S. & TAYLOR, L. (1978) *Prison Secrets*, National Council for Civil Liberties & Radical Alternatives to Prison.
COLMAN, A. (1975) 'The psychology of influence' in *The Tactics of Pressure* (ed. B. Frost), Galliard.
COXALL, W. N. (1981) *Parties and Pressure Groups*, Longman.
CRICK, B. (1959) *The American Science of Politics*, Routledge & Kegan Paul.
CROSSMAN, R. (1977) *The Diaries of a Cabinet Minister*, vol. III, Hamish Hamilton & Jonathan Cape.
DAUBE, M. (1979) 'How to run a pressure group', *Marketing*, Oct.: 75–77.
DAUBE, M. (1981) 'An unhealthy conflict of interests', *Times Health Supplement*, 23 Oct.: 15.
DONNISON, D. (1981) *The Politics of Poverty*, Martin Robertson.
DORFMAN, G. (1974) *Wage Politics in Britain 1945–57*, Charles Knight.
DRINKWATER, C. (1982) 'Planning and the public', *New Society*, 29 April: 182.
FERRIS, P. (1960) *The City*, Victor Gollancz.
FINER, S. E. (1958) *Private Industry and Political Power*, Pall Mall Pamphlet No.3.
FINER, S. E. (1966) *Anonymous Empire*, rev. edn, Pall Mall Press.
FINER, S. E. (1980) *The Changing British Party System, 1945–1979*, American Enterprise Institute.
FITZHERBERT, K. (1982) 'How to protect children in care', *New Society*, 4 Feb.: 180.
FLETCHER, R. (1968) 'Poverty war', *The Guardian*, 21 Oct.: 9.
FLEWIN, J. (1975) 'Cublington Airport' in *The Tactics of Pressure* (ed. B. Frost), Galliard.
FREEMAN, A. (1981) 'Allegations of pressure', *The Times*, 17 Nov.: 2.
FROST, B. (1975) 'The disablement income group' in *The Tactics of Pressure* (ed. B. Frost), Galliard.

GILLARD, M. & TOMKINSON, M. (1980) *Nothing to Declare: The Political Corruptions of John Poulson*, John Calder.

GLYNN, S. & OXBORROW, J. (1976) *Interwar Britain*, Allen & Unwin.

GREGORY, R. (1971) *The Price of Amenity*, Macmillan.

GREY, A. (1975) 'Homosexual law reform' in *The Tactics of Pressure* (ed. B. Frost), Galliard.

GRIFFITH, J. A. G. & STREET, H. (1967) *Principles of Administrative Law*, 4th edn, Isaac Pitman & Sons.

GRIFFITH, J. A. G. (1981) 'Standing Committees in the House of Commons' in *The Commons Today* (ed. S. A. Walkland & M. Ryle), Fontana.

HAGUE, D. C., MACKENZIE, W. J. M. & BARKER, A. (1975) *Public Policy and Private Interests*, Macmillan.

HALL, C. (1974) *How to Run a Pressure Group*, Dent.

HAIN, P. (1971) *Don't Play With Apartheid*, Allen & Unwin.

HERBERT, H. (1978) 'Field tactics', *The Guardian*, 2 Nov.: 13.

HETHERINGTON, A. (1981) 'The lobbyists', *The Listener*, 3 Dec.: 670–1.

HEWART OF BURY, LORD (1929) *The New Despotism*, Benn.

HINDELL, K. & SIMMS, M. (1974) 'How the abortion lobby worked' in *Pressure Groups in Britain: A Reader* (ed. R. Kimber & J. J. Richardson), Dent.

HOGGART, S. & WALLACE, B. (1974) 'A fall in the committee fence', *The Guardian*, 11 May: 11.

HOGGART, S. (1978) 'The manipulators', *The Guardian*, 31 Oct.: 17.

HUNT, N. (1960) 'Early pressure groups, the Russia Company and the Bank of England', *The Listener*, 3 Nov.: 780–2.

IONESCU, G. (1975) *Centripetal Politics*, Hart-Davis.

JACKSON, R.M. (1979) *The Machinery of Justice in England*, 7th edn, Cambridge University Press.

JAY, P. (1970) 'Giving away public assets', *The Times*, 6 Aug.: 21.

JORDAN, A. G. & RICHARDSON, J. J. (1977) 'Outside committees and policy-making: the Central Advisory Water Committee', *Public Administration Bulletin* No. 24 (Aug.) 41–58.

JUDGE, A. (1968) *The First Fifty Years: The Story of the Police Federation*, Police Federation.

JUDGE, D. (1981) *Backbench Specialisation in the House of Commons*, Heinemann.

KIMBER, R. & RICHARDSON, J. J. (1974a) *Pressure Groups in Britain: A Reader*, Dent.

KIMBER, R. & RICHARDSON, J. J. (1974b) 'The Roskillers: Cublington fights the airport' in *Campaigning for the Environment* (ed. R. Kimber & J. J. Richardson), Routledge & Kegan Paul.

KIMBER, R. *et al.* (1974) 'The Deposit of Poisonous Waste Act 1972: a case of government by reaction?', *Public Law* (Autumn): 148–219.

KING, A. (1974) *British Members of Parliament: A Self-Portrait*, Macmillan.

KOGAN, M. & PACKWOOD, T. (1974) *Advisory Councils and Committees in Education*, Routledge & Kegan Paul.

LATHAM, A. (1978) 'The frustrations of lobbying at the House', *The Times*, 27 June: 17.

LATHAM, E. (1965) *The Group Basis of Politics*, Octagon Books.

MCCARTHY, M. A. & MOODIE, R. A. (1981) 'Parliament and pornography: The 1978 Child Protection Act', *Parliamentary Affairs* xxxiv: 47–62.

MACDONALD, D. F. (1976) *The State and the Trade Unions*, 2nd edn, Macmillan.

MCKENZIE, R. T. (1974) 'Parties, pressure groups and the British political process' in *Pressure Groups in Britain: A Reader* (ed. R. Kimber & J. J. Richardson), Dent.

MACKINTOSH, J. P. (1982) *The Government & Politics of Britain* (5th edn, revised by P. G. Richards), Hutchinson.

MADGWICK, P. J. (1976) *Introduction to British Politics*, 2nd edn, Hutchinson.

MANCHESTER, A. H. (1980) *Modern Legal History*, Butterworth.

MARQUAND, D. (1980) *Taming Leviathan: Social Democracy and Centralisation*, Socialist Commentary Publications.

MATHIAS, P. (1958) 'The brewing industry, temperance and politics', *Historical Journal* i: 97–114.

MEDAWAR, C. (1979) *Consumers of Power: Measuring and Improving the Performance of the London Electricity Board*, Social Audit.

MIDDLEMAS, K. (1979) *Politics in Industrial Society*, André Deutsch.

MILLERSON, G. (1964) *The Qualifying Professions*, Routledge & Kegan Paul.

MOODIE, G.C. & STUDDERT-KENNEDY, G. (1970) *Opinions, Publics and Pressure Groups*, Allen & Unwin.

MUIR, R. (1933) *How Britain is Governed*, 3rd edn, Constable.

MULLER, W. D. (1977) *The 'Kept Men'?*, Harvester Press.

NORRIS, J. M. (1957–8) 'Samuel Garbett and the early development of industrial lobbying in Great Britain', *Economic History Review*, Second Series, x: 450–60.

NUGENT, N. (1979) 'The National Freedom Association' in *Respectable Rebels* (ed. R. King & N. Nugent), Hodder & Stoughton.

ODEGARD, P. H. (1958) 'A group basis of politics: a new name for an ancient myth', *Western Political Quarterly* xi: 689–702.
OWEN, J. B. (1974) *The Eighteenth Century 1714–1815*, Nelson.
PENSON, L. M. (1921) 'The London West India interest in the eighteenth century', *English Historical Review* xxxvi: 373–92.
PERKIN, H. (1969) *Key Profession*, Routledge & Kegan Paul.
PINDER, J. (1981) *Fifty Years of Political & Economic Planning*, Heinemann.
PLOWDEN, W. (1971) *The Motor Car and British Politics 1896–1970*, Bodley Head.
POLITICAL & ECONOMIC PLANNING (1960) *Advisory Committees in British Government*, Allen & Unwin.
POLLOCK, S. (1975) *Legal Aid – The First 25 Years*, Oyez Publishing.
POTTER, A. (1957) 'The Equal Pay Campaign Committee: a case-study of a pressure group', *Political Studies* v: 49–64.
POTTER, A. (1961) *Organized Groups in British National Politics*, Faber & Faber.
POWELL, C. & BUTLER, A. (1980) *The Parliamentary and Scientific Committee*, Croom Helm.
PUNNETT, R. M. (1976) *British Government & Politics*, 3rd edn, Heinemann.
PYM, B. (1974) *Pressure Groups and the Permissive Society*, David & Charles.
READ, D. (1964) *The English Provinces c. 1760–1960: A Study in Influence*, Arnold.
REINER, R. (1982) 'Bobbies take the lobby beat', *New Society*, 25 March: 469.
RICHARDSON, J. J. & JORDAN, A. G. (1979) *Governing Under Pressure*, Martin Robertson.
RICHARDSON, J. J. & KIMBER, R. (1972) 'The role of all-party committees in the House of Commons', *Parliamentary Affairs* xxv: 339–49.
ROBERTS, G. K. (1970) *Political Parties and Pressure Groups in Britain*, Weidenfeld.
ROBERTS, G. K. (1971) *A Dictionary of Political Analysis*, Longman.
RUSH, M. (1981) 'Parliament and Government', *Parliamentary Affairs* xxxiv: 463–4.
SANDERSON, J. B. (1974) 'The National Smoke Abatement Society and the Clean Air Act (1956)' in *Campaigning for the Environment* (ed. R. Kimber & J. J. Richardson), Routledge & Kegan Paul.
SELF, P. & STORING, H. (1974) 'The farmers and the state' in *Press-*

ure Groups in Britain: A Reader (ed. R. Kimber & J. J. Richardson), Dent.

SHIPLEY, P. (1979) *Directory of Pressure Groups and Representative Associations*, 2nd edn, Bowker Publishing.

STACEY, F. (1968) *The Government of Modern Britain*, Oxford University Press.

STARKIE, D. (1982) *The Motorway Age: Road and Traffic Politics in Post-war Britain*, Pergamon Press.

STEWART, J. D. (1957) *British Pressure Groups*, Oxford University Press.

TAYLOR, E. (1971) *The House of Commons at Work*, 8th edn, Macmillan.

TRACEY, M. & MORRISON, D. (1979) *Whitehouse*, Macmillan.

TROPP, A. (1957) *The School Teachers*, Heinemann.

TRUMAN, D. B. (1971) *The Governmental Process*, 2nd edn, Alfred A. Knopf.

VAUGHAN, P. (1959) *Doctors' Commons: A Short History of the British Medical Association*, Heinemann.

WADE, H. W. R. (1977) *Administrative Law*, 4th edn, Oxford University Press.

WALKLAND, S. A. (1964) 'Science and Parliament: the origins and influence of the parliamentary and scientific committee', *Parliamentary Affairs* xvii: 389–402.

WEBB, S. & B. (1917) 'Special supplement on professional associations', *New Statesman*, 21 and 28 April.

WIGLEY, J. (1980) *The Rise and Fall of the Victorian Sunday*, Manchester University Press.

WILSON, D. (1967) 'The story of "a triumph" ', *Advertisers' Weekly*, 17 March: 32–5.

WILSON, SIR H. (1976) *The Governance of Britain*, Weidenfeld & Michael Joseph.

WILSON, H. H. (1961) *Pressure Group: The Campaign for Commercial Television*, Secker & Warburg.

WOLFE, J. A. (1915) *Commercial Organisations in the United Kingdom with a description of British Manufacturers' and Employers' Organisations*, USA Bureau of Foreign & Domestic Commerce Special Agents Series No. 102.

WOOTTON, G. (1956) *The Official History of the British Legion*, Macdonald & Evans.

WOOTTON, G. (1970) *Interest-Groups*, Prentice-Hall.

WOOTTON, G. (1975) *Pressure Groups in Britain 1720–1970*, Allen Lane.

WOOTTON, G. (1978) *Pressure Politics in Contemporary Britain*, Lexington Books.

WRAITH, R. (1976) *The Consumer Cause: A Short Account of its Organisation, Development, Power and Importance*, Royal Institute of Public Administration.

YOUNG, J. (1975) 'The aid lobby' in *The Tactics of Pressure* (ed. B. Frost), Galliard.

INDEX